A Youngsters' GUIDE

Prem P. Bhalla

PUSTAK MAHAL®

J-3/16 , Daryaganj, New Delhi-110002
☎ 23276539, 23272783, 23272784 • *Fax:* 011-23260518
E-mail: info@pustakmahal.com • *Website:* www.pustakmahal.com

Sales Centre

- 10-B, Netaji Subhash Marg, Daryaganj, New Delhi-110002
  ☎ 23268292, 23268293, 23279900 • *Fax:* 011-23280567
  E-mail: rapidexdelhi@indiatimes.com
- **Hind Pustak Bhawan**
  6686, Khari Baoli, Delhi-110006
  ☎ 23944314, 23911979

Branches

Bengaluru: ☎ 080-22234025 • *Telefax:* 080-22240209
E-mail: pustak@airtelmail.in • pustak@sancharnet.in
Mumbai: ☎ 022-22010941, 022-22053387
E-mail: rapidex@bom5.vsnl.net.in
Patna: ☎ 0612-3294193 • *Telefax:* 0612-2302719
E-mail: rapidexptn@rediffmail.com
Hyderabad: *Telefax:* 040-24737290
E-mail: pustakmahalhyd@yahoo.co.in

ISBN 978-81-223-0812-9

Edition: 2011

Printed at : Param Offsetters, Okhla, New Delhi-110020

Bhalla's other books

- The Portrait of a **Complete Man**
- **Hello! Just Married or About to Marry?**
- **50 Moral Tales** ...from The Gurukul
- **7 Mantras to Excel in Exams**
- The Book of Etiquette and Manners (Co-author)
- Hindu Rites, Rituals, Customs and Traditions

Author's Note

I have always believed in the ability of our young people. The future depends upon them. They are the future of mankind.

Unfortunately, we have not always provided them the best. The parents are too involved in fulfilling the needs of life. Our education system leaves much to be desired. Adult life presents a picture of double standards.

Faced with this scenario, the young people are confused to find solutions to their problems. Many cannot communicate freely with the parents. Even when the parents are knowledgeable, they are at a loss to talk freely with their children. An informal teacher-student relationship is rare. Friends at school and college may be sailing in the same boat. Yet, the only solution lies in sharing problems and experiences with them. The knowledge that is shared may not be completely authentic or complete. It is of mutual interest. It is the best that is available.

To provide answers to the many questions that bother young people as they grow up, useful information is compiled in a compact form in this book. A variety of subjects are discussed. They range from the problems of growing up to learning to be better individuals and preparing to settle to marry and have a home of their own. Not all the subjects may be of immediate interest to all young people. As they grow up, and face newer problems, they can confidently look forward to find the right answers.

Young people may lack knowledge, but not intelligence or determination. Better informed, I look forward to see young men and women rising as stars of tomorrow. Drawing strength from their loved ones, and from the positive values they have adopted, they bring great hope to this world. To these young men and women, this book is humbly dedicated.

—Prem P. Bhalla

Contents

1

Stepping into the Adult World

"People see what they are prepared to see."

—R.W. Emerson

Every individual steps from childhood into adolescence cherishing great hopes of the adult world that comes into sight. The transition seems to offer an end to parental dependence, a greater opportunity for personal development, and freedom of thought and action. One begins to feel that soon there will be no problems. It would be an easy task to pursue one's goals in life. However, it is not long before one realises that the only problems one is leaving behind are childhood problems. Just as adolescence ushers greater hopes of adult life that awaits every young person, it also brings with it new trials and tribulations.

Nature follows its own pattern. It is not as kind as one would like it to be. The sudden spurt of growth is not uniform. The physical changes cause undue embarrassment. There are marked changes in the skin. Feelings and emotions also begin to be uncertain. While at one time the adolescent bubbles with over-confidence, on another occasion he may want to be as dependent as a child on his parents. There is an inner struggle to get over such personal conflicts, but often it ends up only in frustration.

Parents appear to be no longer as kind as they once were. The circumstances may warrant a showdown with them on many occasions. At the same time, the need to become more responsible becomes urgent. The school and college curriculum demand greater attention. One begins to understand human frailties better through contacts with friends and others. The realities of adult life come to the forefront.

A closer look reveals that adult life is not as attractive as it appeared to be. For the first time, one is shocked to learn the truth about the double standards followed by adults. One comes face to face with the realities of corruption and nepotism, the problems of finding a job, and making a success of it. Money begins to play a greater role as one observes how adult activities revolve around it.

Many of the demands of society are contrary to those of nature. While nature prepares one to be independent, the needs of education for a vocation increase the dependence upon parents until one is self-sufficient to support oneself financially. While nature prepares one to desire sex, to marry, and to procreate, society places restraint upon normal fulfilment of these desires until one is emotionally prepared to shoulder the responsibilities of raising and supporting a family. One begins to realise that marriage is not the happy institution it should be. It entails many problems and sacrifices.

The period of adolescence that represents the transition from childhood into adult life is decidedly a trying period for all young people. While it offers many trials and tribulations, it prepares one to face adult life with confidence. To make this transitory phase of life easier to face, young people need to understand themselves, and the many factors that influence them during this vital phase of life.

Nature has its own way of preparing young people to step into the adult world. During adolescence, it unleashes a spring of hidden energy in each person. There is all round growth. Every portion of the body is stimulated into action with this new energy. The individual is enthusiastic to expend this energy to move on, to achieve greater things in life. This is nature's way of encouraging an individual towards independence in adult life.

It also makes a person over-confident, conceited, and sometimes rash, thus exposing one to hidden dangers. One needs to understand this specially because nature endows all young people with this hidden energy swiftly, but it does not incorporate emotional growth represented by experiences of adult life as rapidly. This necessitates some of the restraints society places upon young people.

How can a young person ensure a happy entry into the adult world? What does one need to do to live a successful life? Young people seek answers to these questions. They need to understand that every stage of life has its own significance. There will be some benefits, but some shortcomings too. At every step one gains valuable experience. The trials of growing up, at times, may be very trying. However, one always overcomes them.

To avoid problems, young people need to listen, to observe, to evaluate, and accept life as it is. Normally, people are afraid of change, and that explains their reluctance to accept new ideas easily. To ensure happiness, one needs to compromise with many things in life.

Habits of a person affect successful living. The foundations of many habits that last a lifetime are built in early childhood. There are many aspects of life and living to which one is exposed only during adolescence. One will do well to understand that making a habit is a simple process. The thought impels one into action. Actions repeated again and again turn into habits. Whether these habits will take one towards success, or failure, depends on whether the initial thoughts were of success or defeat.

This takes young people to the crucial stage where they want to know what is right, and what is not. Many childhood beliefs may be conflicting with those one may come across in the adult world. This can lead to mental conflicts, doubts and frustrations. Many young people may doubt the rationale behind their own existence.

Perhaps never before in the history of mankind were young people more fortunate in that science has taken rapid strides to unravel many mysteries of life. More than ever before, parents and teachers are eager to learn about the needs of young people. Immense knowledge and help is available to guide them to a richer and more successful adult life. The best investment is one a person makes to build oneself. An investment made in knowledge, and in pursuing proper goals, comes back with interest in adult life.

Different aspects of the problem are discussed in detail in the chapters that follow.

Points to ponder...

- ❑ Many demands of nature and those of society are not in harmony with each other.
- ❑ The transition from childhood to adult life is a trying period.
- ❑ At every step, life teaches us something new.
- ❑ Learn to accept life as it is, and not as we would like it to be.
- ❑ The best investment in life is to build oneself through knowledge and work.

❖ ❖

2

The Problems of Growing Up

"In the morning of our days, when the senses are unworn and tender, when the whole man is awake in every part, and the gloss of novelty is fresh upon all the objects that surround us, how lively at that time are our sensations, but how false and inaccurate the judgements we form of things."

—Burke

The process of growing up from childhood to adult life can be very trying for most young people. One undergoes rapid physical and emotional changes. Unable to cope, they go through spells of anxiety. It is a natural part of growing up. Nevertheless, these anxieties can be avoided, if one understands that the developments are natural and normal.

Physical Changes

The most conspicuous change is the sudden spurt in height and weight. Girls begin to grow earlier than boys generally. A girl begins to exhibit physical changes around 11 to 13 years, and a boy around 13 to 15 years. Slight variations are normal and should not arouse undue concern.

In girls, the breasts begin to develop, the hips widen, and hair begins to grow in the pubic region and under the arms.

Sexual maturity is marked by the first experience of menstrual flow. In boys, the penis, testicles and the scrotum develop, shoulders broaden, and hair begins to grow in the pubic area, under the arms, and on the face. The voice deepens. Emission of semen also begins.

Every individual is unique, with inherited characteristics from both the parents. Some begin to grow earlier, and mature sooner too. Height and weight increase may result in one offspring being tall and thin, and another being short and stout. The rapid growth upsets most young people, making them extremely self-conscious. However, by the time one is 20 years old, most of these problems are conveniently over. Even during the difficult period, if one takes active interest in games and social activities, one easily gets over self-consciousness, and learns the ways of adult life.

Changes in the Skin

A problem common to most young people is the occurrence of skin troubles like pimples, blackheads and acne, caused by the imbalance of the levels of hormones in the blood. Another cause is the excess fluid secreted by the sebaceous glands. The sebaceous fluid clogs the skin pores, rendering the skin susceptible to infection.

Cleanliness of the skin is most important. Wash the face with a mild soap and warm water. Rinse with cold water. Dry with a clean towel. Avoid starchy and fatty foods. Consume fruits and vegetables in large quantities to provide vitamins and minerals, which are essential for a healthy skin. These provide useful bulk in the digestive canal. Creams and oily cosmetics aggravate the problem.

Acne normally clears off with maturity. However, if severe, consult a doctor.

The Genitals

Another common anxiety shared by most young people pertains to the genitals. Is the growth normal? What is the new sensation they feel? Why are adults secretive about discussing sex? Such questions often perturb the adolescent.

In boys, the external genitals are the penis and the scrotum, the sac that contains the two testicles. The penis consists of the head, or *glans*, covered with a thin, sensitive and adherent skin, and the shaft covered loosely with thick skin. The penis is formed of erectile tissue. If stimulated, blood rushes into it to make it erect. The size of the genitals is an inherited factor. There is no relationship between one's physique and the size of the genitals. Nor is there any relationship between the size of the genitals and one's ability to enjoy sex in adult life.

In girls, visible externally are only the labia majora, or larger lips, which are wrinkled and covered with hair. When these are pulled apart, one can see the labia minora, or the inner smaller lips, which are of delicate moist skin. At the forward end is the clitoris, which is highly sensitive and erectile, somewhat like the penis in men. Behind the clitoris is the urethra opening for the urine to pass out. Still further inside is the opening of the vagina, which is highly elastic, and leads internally to the uterus. A thin fold of insensitive skin called the hymen partly covers the opening of the vagina in the young girl. Its presence is accepted as proof of her virginity. The hymen is ruptured during the first intercourse and sometimes through games and physical activities.

Menstruation

Nature intends all women become mothers. When a girl experiences her first menstruation marked by the flow of a bloody discharge from the vagina, unless she is properly informed beforehand, say by her mother, she will find its onset a traumatic experience. The start of menstruation indicates that she is ready for childbearing. The periods may be erratic for a year or so. When one begins to get them regularly, they will continue until menopause at the age of around 45 years. She will not get them during pregnancy, or if she has some ailment. It is rare, but if a girl does not get her first period by the time she is 15 years old, she should consult a doctor.

About fourteen days before the onset of the menstrual flow, the ovary produces an ovum (the female reproductive cell). This descends into the uterus in the hope of fertilisation by a sperm (the male reproductive cell). If united, it attaches itself to the wall of the uterus that has simultaneously prepared itself to receive it in the soft lining covering the inside of the uterus. However, when fertilisation does not take place, the lining gradually detaches itself from the uterus, and passes as menstrual flow along with some blood that enters the uterus as the lining detaches itself. The quantity of flow may vary from one time to another. It may last from 3 to 6 days.

Generally the menstrual cycle is of 28 days. It may vary from 21 to 35 days. But once established, menstrual periods are regular.

It is not unusual for some women to be bothered by *premenstrual tension.* This is characterised by a feeling of depression, fatigue and irritability a few days before the onset of the menstrual flow. The breasts may feel heavy and tender, digestion may be disturbed, or there may be general weakness and nervousness. Many times, menstrual periods are accompanied by pain. Sometimes there may be excessive flow. Emotions also have a marked effect upon menstruation. Most of these conditions correct themselves after marriage, but it is the correct attitude about it that is important. It should not cause undue anxiety, or be considered an illness or a curse. It should not restrict normal living. Regular periods reflect good health, and one can indulge in normal activities like going to school, college, or playing games. An elder woman in the family, like the mother or grandmother, should be consulted and their guidance followed.

Nocturnal Emissions

Around the age of 14 or 15, when the male generative organs are developed, a boy may experience his first nocturnal emission, i.e., involuntary ejaculation of semen. He may be aroused from a sexually pleasant dream to find his pajama wet. Thereafter, he may experience nocturnal emissions from time to time. He may be worried that this will affect his health. However, every young man should understand that this is normal.

Sexual Desire

During adolescence young people become aware of the sexual urge—localised in the genitals, although the pleasurable sensations can be felt throughout the body.

Sexual desire differs in men and women. It always begins in the mind, but the response can greatly vary from one time to another. A kiss, an embrace, or even the sight of a nude body may not always arouse desire. At another time, just a thought, the touch of a stranger, a smile, or even the sight of a bare shoulder may spark desire.

Sexual desire in women is different. Whereas girls mature sexually earlier than boys, their actual desire develops much later in the late teens, or sometimes even after they are married. The principal form of stimulation they respond to is touch. In men, the desire is localised in the genitals. In women, it is diffused all over the body. The desire in women also follows a definite cycle linked with the menstrual cycle.

A girl has romantic dreams where she is the beautiful heroine who meets her prince charming. At this stage, she will become conscious of the need for a partner who is a picture of perfection, but rarely is this in the sexual sense. To her, the love of a life-long partner does not primarily mean sexual fulfilment, but involves having a home and being a mother.

It is not true that sexual desire is uncontrollable. Sexual desire in men is at its peak between 16 and 20 years of age. Yet, at this age, society places many restraints making it difficult to find a normal sexual outlet outside marriage. Emotional maturity and financial stability come much later. Many people marry to have uninhibited sexual fulfilment. So as not to allow this desire a free hand in one's life, one needs to learn to sublimate it by way of creative activities, and by taking active part in outdoor activities to keep both the mind and the body occupied.

Finding Sexual Relief

Relief is sought through autoerotism, or masturbation. It is estimated that up to 96 per cent of all adult males indulge in it, at one time or the other. Since sexual relief comes from orgasm marked by the forceful emission of seminal fluid, and is followed by a desire to rest (often confused as weakness), young boys indulge in it with a feeling of shame and guilt. Contrary to what most people believe, masturbation does not cause insanity, affect health, or cause difficulties in making adjustments in adult sexual relationships. It provides relief from sexual tension, but it is devoid of the emotional involvement of a normal sexual relationship between adults.

The incidence of masturbation among girls is comparatively lower. This is because they become aware of their true sexual desire much later. They are not aroused sexually as easily as boys are. Their desire for sexual fulfilment is aroused only when they are stimulated. Therefore, finding sexual relief may not be as urgent for them.

The Trials of Adolescence

During adolescent life, a young person is both a child and an adult. It is undoubtedly a trying situation. One is mature in some ways, and yet not so in others. When one turns to the younger lot for companionship, they consider one rather old to associate with. On the other hand, one is still a child for the older generation.

Since the process of growing up is not uniform in the body, the physical changes make one feel awkward. Outwardly, the appearance of pimples and blackheads, and the growth of breasts in girls, and facial hair and deepening of voice in boys, makes them self-conscious.

Quarrels with parents and others are common, though they may be accompanied with feelings of guilt.

This is a time when young persons need to be reassured that all is normal. Every person has gone through this stage. There is no need for any anxiety about it. Give group activities the importance they rightly deserve. Parents always have the welfare of their children uppermost in their minds, and can be your best friends.

Growing up Emotionally

Unlike physical growth, emotional growth does not come automatically as a natural process of growing up and is a slow process dependent upon one's ability to convert personal experiences to personal benefit. Emotional maturity comes with stability in one's thoughts and actions.

Many values of life are learnt early in childhood as one watches and assesses parents and others in the household. A wide new world opens as one steps into adult life, giving every person an opportunity to compare values. Experiences come slowly. As one evaluates them, and stores all useful knowledge in the mind, one grows emotionally and this helps withstand the storms of adult life later.

Points to ponder...

- ❑ The anxieties of growing up are normal.
- ❑ The variations in growing patterns are normal.
- ❑ Understand your physical self.
- ❑ Understand your emotions and feelings.
- ❑ Understand the new adult emerging from a grown-up child.
- ❑ Learn to direct yourself intelligently.

3

Developing Personal Charm

> ***"The shortest and surest way to live with honour in the world is to be in reality what we would appear to be."***
>
> **—Socrates**

It is natural for everyone to desire to look attractive. This desire keeps a person alert to the need for projecting a good image of oneself in society. People go to great lengths to achieve this. Some succeed, but many do not. It becomes significant as one steps into adolescence and feels the need to be accepted by society as an individual. Many factors influence the image one projects in everyday life.

What Makes a Person Attractive?

A person appears attractive when he, or she, possesses certain qualities which delight the eye, or the mind. If one is blessed with a charming set of features or a smooth, attractive skin, it is a great asset to draw immediate attention, but qualities which make one truly attractive come from within. However, once they are cultivated gradually through consistent effort, they become a part of a person.

Everything, be it good or bad, begins with a thought. It is the same with personal charm also. Since the face is an index of the mind, to look attractive we must be at peace with ourselves. Our thoughts, actions and habits must aim at the higher values of life. Through them, we enrich our character, and this in turn makes one attractive.

A smiling face reflects inner peace and happiness. Posture and carriage also contribute to personal attractiveness. A gentle voice and good manners enhance personal charm.

Finally, one cannot overlook the need to dress well. Clothes help to attract immediate attention, and reflect one's personal tastes. Elegance does not necessarily come from expensive clothes. Clean, crisp clothes worn without much fuss are both comfortable and attractive.

Developing Personal Charm

Two aspects of personal attractiveness need consideration. Firstly, it is the external appearance. Secondly, the charm and radiance that comes from within.

An attractive external appearance may come as a gift of nature as each individual is born unique. Some are blessed with beautiful features at birth. The external beauty endowed by nature is of little use unless it can regularly draw from the reservoir of power-giving qualities that come from within. The charm that the face and the body reflect comes from good physical and emotional health. External cleanliness is of great importance. A smiling face, a pleasing and rhythmic voice, one's poise and manners all add to one's personal charm.

Everything begins with a thought. Thoughts turn into actions. These actions, when repeated, turn into habits. Our habits cumulatively reflect what we believe in, and what we are. Our thoughts are either positive (constructive), or negative (destructive). A thought is positive if it is useful in a given situation, and negative if it is not. When the mind is fed with positive thoughts, one develops personal magnetism. However, if one entertains negative thoughts, there is corresponding loss of power.

Why is it that most people fail to develop positive thinking to the desired level? Is it that positive thinking is difficult to practise? No, it is not so. In fact, it takes no more effort to do positive thinking than it does to do negative thinking! The real problem lies with the individual. Before one can develop personal magnetism, one must believe in one's personal ability to develop it. With a high incidence of negativity in the environment, most people fail to reach their goal.

To develop personal charm, believe in your capabilities. Follow the simple rules of good health. Stay as close to nature as you can. Observe self-discipline as it gives strength of character. Learn to get along with people. Develop wider interests in life. Make self-improvement a regular part of your everyday life. Screen your thoughts so that only positive thoughts take hold of you. Keep yourself in a high state of enthusiasm through a fair balance between work and recreation. Gradually you will find that you develop greater inner peace and personal charm.

Beauty Aids

The markets are flooded with beauty aids of varied descriptions making all sorts of claims to make one beautiful and attractive. Although most of them are for ladies, there are many for men too. Since people of both the sexes are eager to look attractive, these preparations interest and attract everyone. Not all preparations are good.

The best beauty aids are a good toilet soap and clean cold water. Together these ensure cleanliness, which is the primary ingredient for developing personal charm. It is better that young women use light make-up, and have simple hairstyles to produce a natural alluring effect. As a part of make-up, the application of a foundation followed by a good face powder, and lipstick to match the complexion, hair and clothes creates a good effect. Avoid eye make-up. If you must use it, do so sparingly. Short nails with nail polish of natural shade are practical and look good. Regular hair care is as important as care of the skin. The most important thing is to establish a beauty routine where one is conscious of the need for good health, exercise, balanced food, cleanliness, sufficient rest and sleep.

Young men need not be as fastidious about cosmetics as ladies. However, the rules of cleanliness and good grooming hold true for everyone. No young man who wants to look attractive can ignore the need for periodic dental care, regular shaves and regular trimming of the nails and hair. These reflect one's personal sense of grooming. Many beauty aids are made especially for men. These have a positive masculine flavour and fragrance. One need not feel shy to use these.

The Wardrobe

Dress as well as you can afford to. Clothes help one draw immediate attention and reflect one's taste. The colour sets the mood. Various colours influence one differently. Some are cool and pacifying, others warm and stimulating. One can take advantage of this by wearing clothes that are in harmony with one's personality.

Expensive clothes are not necessary. They must be comfortable to wear, easy to maintain and elegant to look at. The stitching, styles and fitting are important. These can make or mar the beauty of the finest fabrics. A quality which is most appreciated in any wardrobe is its adaptability to give the impression of plenty. To make the wardrobe so versatile is really an art.

Before buying clothes for yourself, assess your needs. Visualise the utility of the clothes you are going to buy. Ask yourself if you are buying them because you need them, or you are only supplementing your existing wardrobe. Do not buy too many clothes at a time. When you buy a few from time to time, you can be certain of keeping up with the changing trends in fashion and styles.

Etiquette in Everyday Life

Just as a lubricant helps to move machine parts smoothly, so do good manners and etiquette help one to move amongst people winning goodwill and understanding. A simple guiding thought in one's everyday life should be consideration for others' feelings. We come across many people from different vocations everyday. A smiling face and a genial temperament help win goodwill everywhere. When one is sincere, with time it becomes habitual.

The simple courtesies of being punctual for appointments, of greeting a person when you meet, or of saying "sorry", "excuse me", "thank you", etc., may appear trifling in themselves, but these immediately reflect one's sincerity of purpose. Such courtesies do not need to be reserved for elders or superiors only. Extend them to all without any distinction.

The courtesy of a 'thank you' note, or a greeting card at Diwali, Christmas, or New Year helps renew acquaintance, and win goodwill.

Points to ponder...

- ❑ Everyone desires to be attractive.
- ❑ Nature intends all to be beautiful.
- ❑ Real personal charm comes from within.
- ❑ Clothes must be comfortable to wear and elegant to look at.
- ❑ Good etiquette immediately wins goodwill and understanding.

❖❖

4

The Pursuit of Education

"Education is not learning; it is the exercise and development of the powers of the mind; and the two great methods by which this end may be accomplished are in the halls of learning, or in the conflicts of life."

—Princeton Review

It is surprising to note the large number of young people who study in schools and colleges without the least idea as to why they are doing it. Most of them feel that a diploma or degree will be a promotional aid in life, but are not sure how getting educated can help them. Is it then surprising that they do not do well? Our schools and colleges are full of students who physically visit the educational institutions regularly, but do not derive benefits from them. This not only affects individual prospects of successful adult life, but when added together, it results in millions of wasted hours, disillusionment and unhappiness. A correct attitude towards this vital aspect of life can help one get ahead successfully.

What is Education?

What does education mean to you? A good schooling? A degree? Alternately, perhaps a diploma in some craft? To most young people education is one of these things. They heave a sigh of relief as soon as they pass through school and college, and end up with sufficient certificates that they can use as a passport to a good job. The better the school and college career, the better the chances of a well-paid job. To most young men education is the means of getting a job, and to young women it means better prospects of finding a good husband.

The word 'education' is derived from the Latin word *educare*, which means 'to rear'. Education, therefore, is the process of preparing a person to use personal capabilities buried deep within each one. A certificate, diploma or degree is no more than a paper that certifies a particular person has undergone a certain level of study. However, since not many young people can use the knowledge so gained to personal advantage, the very purpose of such education becomes futile.

Schooling is a medium of passing certain fixed ideas into the minds of growing young people. To a certain extent, this is essential in modern society. However, true education begins where mass schooling ends. It is not enough to learn to speak, read or write. It is also not enough to study the languages, science or art, or anything else as a separate entity. Each one of them has a definite purpose. However, none of them can be useful unless they help in developing a person as a whole as he needs to live in society. The early training should become the foundation of the true form of education. Through it, one should learn to bring forth from within the ideas that benefit the individual, and mankind. Such education helps one to become creative and, through a wider outlook of life, develop a personality which is out of the ordinary.

Life in School and College

All young people find life in school and college rather arduous, but the time spent in school, and later in college, represent the most memorable years of life. During this period one gains not only valuable knowledge to pursue a successful career in life, but also gathers those vital memories that make life richer. Many of the friendships that develop during this period last a lifetime.

The very concept of mass schooling is beginning to be challenged by some thinkers, as it tends to stifle individual creative thinking, and produces stereotyped thinkers. There are no immediate alternatives available to accept and follow. The foundation of higher learning is laid in school. Gradually, as an individual begins to understand personal needs, the superstructure is cast.

Unfortunately, with most schools and colleges overcrowded, ill-equipped and lacking in many basic requirements of a good educational institution, most young people are unable to reap the benefits of wholesome school and college life. Of course many of these shortcomings cannot be easily made up for, but it is not rare to find enterprising young people getting together to arrange and enjoy many extra- curricular activities like games, social get-togethers and the like.

Going to College

Although our colleges are overcrowded, unfortunately, most young people do not properly utilise their education. The truth is that these people should not have gone to college in the first place. Many of them go just because everyone else is doing so. It affords them an opportunity to meet and know a variety of people from different sections of society. This in itself does help widen their outlook. However, with their lack of interest in studies, there are chances that such contacts may often have an adverse effect. The entire effort may go waste.

If you think you need college education, ask yourself why you need it. Look back at your past academic achievements. Have they been above average? Do you think that you will benefit by going to college? Ask your parents and friends. A college education is for those who have a definite purpose for it in life. The mental development of a college student must be above average. There should be a strong desire to learn. Financial requirements need to be considered. This is best discussed with parents.

College education needs planning ahead of time. One must decide what kind of college one wants to study in. Most colleges offer only graduation courses, but there are many which offer vocational courses for both men and women. Get information about the colleges that interest you as early as possible. Find out about entrance requirements, the period of study, the diploma or degree awarded, job training provided after the course, and other such pertinent information that can help you in selecting the right course and college. You need to apply for admission well in time. Many colleges have prescribed forms to make an application for admission. Wherever necessary, you can supplement the information required on a separate sheet of paper to list your past academic achievements, subjects studied, any special remarks, recommendations and reports from your past teachers, and your co-curricular and extra-curricular achievements, if any.

Studying Effectively

Whether it is at school, college, or elsewhere, the only way to gain knowledge is to study the subject effectively. However, why is it that some people grasp whatever they study rather quickly, while most people have to struggle hard to understand the subject? This often perplexes youngsters in schools and colleges. The difference is certainly not because one set is luckier than the rest. Nor is it that these few are a specially blessed lot. In reality the difference lies in the simple fact that those who grasp and understand their subject matter quickly are those who follow certain simple rules of making the best of what they learn. All young people can follow their example.

Successful students have an inquisitive mind, are confident of their ability, are regular, and genuinely interested in their work. To be a successful student, learn to be eager about your work. If you are not interested in learning a particular subject, no amount of coaxing can make it a part of you. To avoid such indifference on your part, you will need to keep yourself in a high state of motivation by constantly reminding yourself how this study is going to benefit you. The greater your interest in the subject, the sooner you will master it.

Few people are good in all subjects. Do not let it discourage you if you like some subjects, and are weak in others. The important thing is that while you will need to develop the ones that you like, you will also need to pay special attention to those in which you may be weak. Find out why you are weak in these subjects, and what can be done to improve your performance here.

One way of learning your subject quickly is to simplify it. Make notes of what you learn. Writing your work offers an opportunity to ponder over the subject longer, and gradually fix it in the mind. Gather all the facts that you can by asking yourself what, when, why, how, where and which about the subject matter. Put facts in the correct order, and visualise them in terms of what you already know to create picture images in your mind. Memorising what you learn may appear simpler, but it is not so. It is a sure way to confusion. Instead, try to understand the facts. Revise your work often. Consult as many books on the subject as you can. The deeper your study and understanding of the subject, the better your performance.

No student who wishes to learn something can afford to overlook the help teachers can give. Never hesitate to ask them about your doubts and difficulties. Many students feel that others may laugh at their ignorance, and therefore prefer to keep their doubts to themselves. This is a wrong thing to do. Curiosity and an intelligent approach are always appreciated by teachers.

Getting Along with Teachers

Teachers are an indispensable part of the process of learning. Some are immediately likeable, others are not. Some are efficient, others are not. Nevertheless, they are reasonable. As a student, one should only be concerned with the benefit from the knowledge they can impart.

Many students entertain a mental image of what a teacher should be, and finding that one does not come up to this ideal they have in mind, lose confidence in him. Soon one's own work begins to suffer. It is difficult to find ideal teachers just as it is difficult to find perfect pupils. Like everyone else, teachers have their own problems and frustrations. These should be of no concern to the student.

Learning Aids

Every successful student pursues his work through the aid of good notes. Notes can be made of the important points discussed in the lecture. These can be elaborated later at home, with special emphasis on understanding the basic matter that has been taught. Organising study groups for a better understanding of the subjects helps in fixing ideas in the mind firmly. You could have such groups at the school or college level, but if it is not possible, then it is still worth the while to have a group of friends who can study together.

Another source of knowledge is your school, college or public library. All students who have taken their work seriously consult books related to the matter of study. To derive the maximum benefit from the library, set aside some time regularly to visit it. Understand what titles are available. Take the assistance of the librarian in-charge.

Appearing for Examinations

There are two aspects of appearing for examinations. Firstly, preparing oneself for the examination; secondly, the examination itself.

To achieve success positively, one must work ahead of time. There is no substitute for regular work. Do not try to break new ground just before the examinations. Only revise what you know. Memorisation can only add to the confusion.

Understand the basic concepts and ideas. Visualise words and sentences as pictures. If you have prepared notes earlier, revision becomes an easy and simple affair. Assure yourself of a full night's sleep before the examination. Avoid tension. Keep yourself composed as that improves performance.

When the examination begins, read the question paper carefully, taking particular note of special instructions, if any, on the top of the question paper. Budget your time. Answer the questions you know best first. Tackle the ones you are unsure about last. Be careful about your grammar, spellings and punctuation. Present your answers methodically. Illustrate the answers with neat diagrams where necessary. Keep the answers brief, and to the point. If a portion is to be cancelled, do it as neatly as you possibly can. The overall appearance of the answer paper must be neat.

Making Up Lost Time

What one studies in schools and colleges only helps in providing a strong foundation. The real education comes from a personal effort made in the right direction. One can start at any time in life. Provided one is willing to learn, and continues to persevere, there is no reason why one cannot develop personal capabilities of the highest level.

Many opportunities exist in every town to widen the horizon of one's interests. Refresher courses, short-term courses, evening classes, public libraries, hobby clubs, and such facilities are intended to improve personal capabilities. In smaller towns where such facilities are still not fully developed, correspondence courses and personal study offer a wide avenue of learning that can be very beneficial.

Specialised magazines, newspapers, discussion groups, seminars, and similar get-togethers can be helpful in increasing one's knowledge.

A Balanced Education

In every sphere of life, there is an emphasis on specialisation. So it is natural for every young person to endeavour to gain the maximum knowledge on the subject of his study. However, in practical everyday life, this form of specialisation has its limitations. Successful living, which is the ultimate aim of every individual, cannot be narrowed down to a single subject of specialised study. It is the success in small day-to-day events of life that adds up to become bigger successes. To achieve this, one requires a wide knowledge of several subjects. It is the sum total of these, which reflects how educated a person is. The education must be balanced to promote both physical and emotional development, which enables a person to face the challenges of everyday life.

Education — an Ongoing Process

Knowledge on every subject continues to grow every day. The sum total of knowledge in the world doubles every ten years. Under such circumstances, it is certainly not possible to keep up with every detail of growing knowledge. However, if one were to stop adding something new to one's knowledge regularly, it would not be long before one is left behind.

Most young people feel that with the end of their schooling, or a few years in college, their days of learning are over. Nothing could be further from the truth. People who entertain such thoughts have rarely reached the peak of their mental development, and should not hope for any further growth. On the other hand, a progressive person continues to expand the horizons of knowledge. It does not matter whether one learns something new about his subject of specialisation, or something that would be useful in life. Provided one has an open mind, and is on the lookout for knowledge that can be beneficial, there is no end to learning. A progressive person knows that education is an ongoing process.

Points to ponder...

- ❑ Good education aims at developing a complete person.
- ❑ Use education to build yourself.
- ❑ Plan education to lead you to a successful career.
- ❑ Successful students study effectively.
- ❑ Aim for a balanced education.
- ❑ Education is an ongoing process.

5

Getting Along with Parents

"How many hopes and fears, how many ardent wishes and anxious apprehensions, are twisted together in the threads that connect the parent with the child!"

—S.G. Goodrich

Not many young people claim to enjoy perfect understanding with their parents. In fact, most of them are not satisfied with them at all. We cannot overlook that this is not a problem of recent origin. It has existed since times immemorial. Even our forefathers felt the same way about their parents.

Young people feel that parents are too conservative in their outlook, lack understanding, and above all else are authoritarian and dictatorial. The parents too have their grievances about the young people. They feel that youngsters are irresponsible, headstrong, and desire more freedom and independence of thought and action than is good for them. Besides, they are unhappy about youngsters' disregard for established values. Young people emphasise that they are educated, can differentiate good from bad, and have a right to express themselves as individuals. Again, the parents stress that they know better because they have passed through youth.

The confidence that the youth express is not based upon experience, but only upon enthusiasm common at their age.

Which of the two is right, it is difficult to conclude immediately. Both the young and the parents are firm about their opinion. Their arguments are based upon personal feelings and experiences. However, the parent-child relationship is of vital importance to everyone. We need to understand the underlying problems better. The problems must be resolved, and the relationship made mutually satisfying to both the younger and the older generation.

The Generation Gap

An easy way to explain the differences between the two generations has been found. People call it the generation gap. Does such a gap really exist? Or, is it something imaginary? The term 'generation gap' is of recent origin.

The truth is that there always have been differences of opinion between the young and the old. What great sages and philosophers said about this relationship hundreds of years ago is as applicable today, as it was when they first said it. The times have changed, the environments have changed, but human nature has continued to remain the same. The young people of today will be parents in a few years. Perhaps there would still be the same differences of opinion between them and their children. Similar anxieties will perplex them.

However, life can be rewarding when we try to resolve problems by understanding the parent-child relationship a little better.

The Parent-Child Relationship

Many young people feel that their birth has been more a matter of chance than of choice, and perhaps that explains the differences between the two generations. Even if such a contention of youngsters was true, the differences can not be explained so easily. The parent-child relationship is a very deep-rooted relationship. With many factors affecting it, the complexities make it unpredictable.

Whether a child is born by chance or by choice, from the very beginning certain bonds between the child and the parents, particularly the mother, begin to grow. Whether the child likes it or not, it inherits characteristics from the parents. This is controlled by nature, and nobody can exert a choice over it. Again, when a child is born, he immediately comes under the influence of his parents. Since it is natural for the parents to relive their childhood through their offspring, they bring it under the influences that they feel are best by their standards. Of course, what is good, and what is not, depends upon individual concepts and preferences.

The main cause of parents' concern is that adolescence is a difficult period for all young people, who cannot readily accept the physical and emotional changes that come over them rather suddenly. Besides, while the physical development is rapid, emotional growth is not so. The imbalance makes one rash in judgement of men and matters. Since adolescence means the entry from childhood to the adult world, curiosity and the spirit of experimentation in new circumstances can also land young people into trouble.

This is also a time when the young people are gradually breaking off from parents, and learning to develop new relationships with other young people of both sexes. These relationships can be vital in that they exert varied influences that can make or mar adult values and habits for a lifetime. Many of these anxieties are easily overcome if the parents and the young people can effectively communicate with each other.

Communicating with Parents

Effective communication should not pose any difficulty provided young people can understand their parents' concern, and parents can understand the needs of their children. The problem with most of us is that we take too much for granted. We twist the meaning of incoming messages to suit our personal convenience, and expect that the other party be fully capable of understanding what we are trying to convey. Both these attitudes lead to ineffective communication.

Since life is dynamic, and views and concepts continue to change with time, harmony at home can come only from a two-way communication with parents. To make it possible, young people need to make a positive effort to understand the viewpoint of parents. At the same time, it will be necessary to provide parents an opportunity to understand youngsters well. Brooding over something is of no avail. If you feel strongly about something, it would be helpful if you can discuss it with your parents. They may contradict you, but they have your interests in mind.

Winning Your Parents' Cooperation

When you want your parents to cooperate with you, you will need to cooperate with them first. Before you can understand them, you will need to understand yourself. Any good relationship depends upon mutual goodwill and thoughtfulness about each other's feelings. Goodwill cannot be created overnight. Gaining it is a slow process.

What the parents consider good, and what they do not, is often very difficult to understand for most young people. This is particularly so because many adults follow dual standards in their everyday life. They preach one thing, and practise quite another. There is no harm if you rationally explain your viewpoint to them. Such communications promote mutual goodwill and better understanding.

You will do well to show your parents what you are capable of. Take up responsibilities, and fulfil them to their satisfaction. Very often the responsibilities of everyday life appear too insignificant to exhibit one's capabilities, but it is not so. Small achievements prepare one for successes that are more important later. Each little success prepares one for a greater one the next time. Eventually one is ready to handle the most responsible positions in life.

A Code of Conduct

To ensure that the spirit of cooperation between the young and their parents is effective, there is always the need for a code of conduct about which both parties should be aware of. This is very necessary as young people may indulge in certain activities rather innocently without a thought that parents may be offended or hurt. Of course any such code of conduct must necessarily be flexible, and will vary for youth across various sections of society, but the basic values of any such code will be common, and must be given due consideration.

A subject of great concern to all parents is their children's friends. They desire that their children should have friends who come from families that share similar values as they do. All youngsters feel that they have good people as friends. It is, therefore, best that parents get to know the friends. Due to various factors, it is not easy for young people to ascertain how their friendships will turn out. Therefore, the best rule to follow is to have such friends whom you can unhesitatingly bring home to meet your parents. This way, several people screen a person simultaneously. By bringing your friends closer to the family, you can develop relationships that are more informal.

Going out with friends to their homes, or a picnic, or a movie, should normally not arouse any misunderstanding. However, considering how concerned parents can be, it would only be in the fitness of things that you inform them where you are going, with whom, and when they could expect you to return home. If you are delayed due to certain unavoidable reasons, it is a simple courtesy that you immediately inform them on telephone that you will be late. This is of particular significance when young girls go out alone with their friends. If she is to stay out late, she must be escorted home safely.

There is also great need for a definite understanding between young people and parents about bringing home their friends for meals. Some parents do not mind it, but many positively object to it. Every family must settle the issue for themselves. But a good rule for young people is that if they cannot call a friend home for an informal meal, do not impose yourself on others.

Since a party is a planned function, it is bound to be in consultation with the parents. They may not insist about checking the list of invitees, but you will need to be careful about your parents' views on smoking or drinking by you or your friends on such occasions. The entertainment programmes like dancing, party games, etc., that you arrange should also be in keeping with the established norms and values acceptable to your parents.

The use of the family telephone and vehicle (scooter or car) often cause great misunderstandings between young people and parents. You need to remember that these are conveniences for everyone to use, and not monopolise. Since the parents' contacts and needs are bound to be greater than yours, give them the opportunity to avail of these facilities. Do not hesitate to make this clear even to your friends who may call you on the telephone. Your needs are only next in importance to the needs of your parents, and therefore it is just right that the needs must be flexible and reasonable.

Another vital matter of dissent between young people and parents is that of spending money. Some parents are rather liberal, but most of them cannot afford to be. Pocket allowances vary amongst people from different sections of society. As a rule, one should learn to live within the limitations this places upon each one of us. If you must spend more than what your parents can afford, you must deserve this extra allowance by either bringing about certain economies in the running of the home, or by earning it through a part-time job.

Points to ponder...

- ❑ Many young people are not completely satisfied about the relationships with their parents.
- ❑ Differences of opinion between the young and their parents have always existed.
- ❑ The parent-child relationship is much stronger than what we imagine it to be.
- ❑ One must try to understand parents' concerns.
- ❑ Effective communication brings down barriers.
- ❑ Adopt a code of conduct acceptable to you and your parents.

❖❖

6

Money in Everyday Life

"Money does all things, for it gives and it takes away, it makes honest men and knaves, fools and philosophers; and so on to the end of the chapter."

—L'Estrange

Even a child knows the function of money. If s/he gets a coin, s/he will buy a candy or a balloon. The child also knows that money is required to buy things. When children start going to school, some parents give their wards pocket money. Thus the idea of pocket money has become widely prevalent.

Children should be taught the need for thrift-proper use and conservation of money. The saving habit should be inculcated from an early age. The ideal would be to open a minor account in the bank in the name of the child and persuade him/her to deposit at least part of one's pocket money. The child can be made to understand that invested spare money will earn by way of interest. If there are two or more children in the household, a competitive spirit could be inculcated.

Children are likely to buy eatables like candy or popcorn with their pocket money. It is not safe to consume eatables from a street vendor or stall. It may not be hygienic and could result in infection. Children should be made aware of the health hazards. It will then help them to save.

The financial position of a family reflects in the attitude of its members towards money. Rich people are indifferent and liberal in their spending habits. Poor parents struggling to make both ends meet are not able to hide the real situation from their children. If parents take the young members into confidence about their background, children will understand that they cannot ask for more money or spend it as they please.

Once they realise the value of money and the need for thrift, they will be careful in all money transactions whether their own (like buying books and other school requirements) or that of the family.

They may become dishonest when they develop vices like smoking or bunking classes to see a movie and face shortage of funds. They may then be tempted to steal.

In his autobiography, Gandhiji narrates how he, as an adolescent, fell into bad company and took to smoking surreptitiously and to procure funds for it, he even stole money. Of course, he had strong character and came out of the snare unscathed. Every young person should read this absorbing account of Gandhiji's life.

Adolescents and adults of middle class or poor families can augment their resources by taking on odd jobs like delivering newspapers and other services. This, besides bringing in some much-needed money, also inculcates in them the dignity of labour.

They can open their own savings accounts in banks which allow minors to open and operate accounts. Once they make a beginning, experience will teach them good habits like having pass books, cheque books, maintaining minimum balance, opening a recurring deposit account and investing in term deposits even for small amounts as the savings grow.

When they grow up, they will also know that one has to work to earn and one's education is primarily meant to enable one to take up a profession or employment. Once they realise how money can empower them to possess various things and spend on luxuries and entertainment, it would serve as an incentive to pursue their education diligently and obtain degrees or diplomas which will secure for them remunerative employment, leading ultimately to financial security.

Young people should consider the pitfalls of unenlightened chasing of money and acquire a proper perspective regarding finance and allied matters. A miser attracts social odium. A profligate will end up a pauper. Money is a good servant, but a bad master.

Points to ponder...

- ❑ Money plays an important part in everday life.
- ❑ Understand the different aspects of money.
- ❑ Money puts everyone's honesty and integrity to test.
- ❑ Learn to get the best out of money.
- ❑ Monetary values are learnt in childhood.
- ❑ A good understanding of money promotes financial satisfaction.

❖❖

7

Personal Health

"To preserve health is a moral and religious duty, for health is the basis of all social virtues. We can no longer be useful when not well."

—Johnson

Young people are generally not anxious about health. Nevertheless, all of them do want to enjoy good health. Young people are specially blessed by nature as regards health. They are still growing physically. There is a bountiful supply of energy from within. Setbacks in health, if any, are quickly repaired.

Good health comes from having the right habits and attitudes in life. Once these have crystallised during childhood and adolescence, changes in the later years may be difficult to make. An understanding of the subject can therefore be beneficial to young people to enable them to face health problems in adult life boldly.

What is Good Health?

A person is said to be healthy when he is happy, eats well, eliminates the waste products regularly, meets his everyday responsibilities without undue strain, and sleeps well to meet the challenges of yet another day. Doctors declare a person physically fit when his pulse, breathing, temperature and blood pressure are normal. Health is also considered in terms of body weight as linked to height, and with the absence of a feeling of strain and fatigue. To satisfy these necessities of good health, it is important that the various systems in the body function in harmony with each other, and be governed by a sound mind.

The Human Body

The human body is an intricate combination of several body functions dependent upon each other for harmonious operation. While the bones provide the basic framework, the muscles (with some fat) provide the padding, and enable it to move. The skin acts as the outer covering to hold everything together. The nutrients to fuel growth, and to repair the wear and tear of the body tissues, come from the digestive system. The requirements of air are provided by the respiratory system. The circulatory system helps to carry the nutrients through the blood to wherever they are required. It also helps to carry the waste products from various parts of the body to the excretory system to be eliminated as urine or sweat. The defence mechanism of the body protects it from harmful germs that we come in contact with as we eat, drink or move about. The nervous system controls all the functions of the body.

Nature has made the human body an almost foolproof machine. It is capable of bearing great stress and strain and can withstand many kinds of disabilities. However, we cannot overlook one important fact. Each individual is born unique, each person may respond differently to similar circumstances.

The maintenance of good health, therefore, continues to remain a very personal matter.

Understanding Yourself

Each person has to evaluate personal needs and responses to the living conditions. Nature has intended to make the human body perfect. However, in practical everyday life when it is exposed to the stress of varying types, some tension builds up. If this is not relieved intelligently, certain functions in the body may be deranged. Nature has a way of giving stress signals to warn a person to be careful. An early adjustment in the way of living can help get over them. Since some problems may be inherited, when beyond human control, the only remedy lies in learning to live with them. Experience has shown that people with even serious setbacks to health live to a ripe old age when they are careful. When a person feels that stress signals given by the body mean nothing, a mild problem may soon become a serious setback. Nature is kind. However, when abused, it spares no one.

Health Consciousness

Nature has endowed everyone with the right to live a healthy and fruitful life. However, every individual must exercise this right by developing health consciousness. Since the mind is the master control centre of the body, this can be achieved by feeding the mind with the right kind of thoughts. When you want to be healthy, you will need to feed the mind with thoughts of good health. Think of good health. Talk of good health. Learn to be happy. Happiness and good health are inter-connected. When you become conscious of the need for good health, you automatically begin to think of the many factors that make or mar your health. Learn to use those that benefit you, and eliminate those that do not. The correct attitudes and habits continue to help one throughout life.

Factors Affecting Health

As we have seen, nature has tried to make the human body almost perfect. However, certain basic needs must be provided to keep it functioning well. It needs protection from the vagaries of the environment. It must get the correct form of nutrition and exercise. Waste products must be cleansed from the system regularly. These needs are rather simple, but when it comes to providing them, one tends to make many mistakes.

One must regularly be on a balanced diet rich in protein, with some carbohydrates and a little fat. Milk, fruits and vegetables that provide bulk and essential vitamins and minerals must form a good portion of the diet. Eat food unhurriedly, and chew it thoroughly. Avoid work and worry at mealtimes. Do not overeat. More people suffer in adult life due to overeating than any other cause. Eating snacks and drinking beverages should never replace regular meals. It is also useful to remember that one tends to be indiscriminate about eating at parties. Do not ignore the importance of drinking lots of water every day.

Just as important as the food we eat is the need of fresh air for the body. The larger the capacity of our lungs, and the deeper we breathe, the more oxygen we provide to the body. Deep breathing is very stimulating. We cannot also overlook the need for ample exercise for the body as this promotes better breathing and circulation of blood. Exercise ensures an even distribution of fat all over the body, giving it a well-proportioned appearance.

Indigestible matter along with some undigested food is eliminated through bowel movements. Waste products from various parts of the body are excreted through urine, and partly through perspiration. A missed bowel movement should not cause anxiety, as the cause may be lack of sufficient roughage in the diet. It will also be useful to remember that passing of urine is affected by weather and emotions. One passes more urine when frightened, worried and during cold weather. Drinking sufficient water ensures this body function is in good order.

Finally, the need for adequate rest cannot be overemphasised to maintain good health. Brief periods of rest in the day and good sound sleep at night provide renewed energy and strength to face the challenges of life.

Emotional Health

Since the mind controls all body functions, one cannot expect to be physically healthy unless one is emotionally healthy. The two are completely interlinked. It is not enough to provide the body with the right kind of nutrition, exercise and fresh air. We must feed the mind too. The problem here is that even without any effort on our part, the mind is fed with thoughts of varying kinds. Life is a series of compromises made each day with our environments and circumstances. A certain amount of stress continues to promote tension within us all the time. This stress is very different from physical stress that is immediately recognised, and finds relief through rest and sleep. Emotional stress continues to build up even without the least physical exertion, and can affect one at any time. Still worse, it is habit forming.

Therefore, it is essential that one learn to cope with this type of stress. In the first place, one should try to slow the build up of emotional stress through a positive outlook towards life and its problems. Secondly, it must find regular relief through recreation. A happy mind ensures a healthy body.

The Family Doctor

Despite the best care, at times one may not feel well. Under such circumstances, do not avoid consulting your family doctor. He can be your best friend. Even when you feel it is nothing serious, consulting him about a complaint will help set your mind at rest about any anxieties that may bother you. In good health too, it is useful to keep in touch with your family doctor. More than anything else, it keeps a person aware of the need to be health conscious, and to know where to call in case of need.

Tonics and Drugs

With the large-scale growth of advertising and availability of tonics and drugs at all chemists and druggists, many people fall an easy prey to experimenting with them to keep healthy. Unless used on the recommendation of a qualified doctor, this is a wrong thing to do. Most of the time they are not needed at all. They produce temporary stimulation or rest, and the relief may only come from the fulfilment of the psychological craving that a tonic or drug has been taken. Some of these are habit forming. Others may produce immunity to certain drugs that may need to be administered in an emergency. Some drugs can have serious side effects also. In view of these dangers, it is best to avoid the use of tonics or drugs without a doctor's prescription.

A Plan for Living

The secret of good health ultimately means no more than adopting and following a plan for living. Discipline in every sphere of life gives strength. It is the same with health. Since health is a personal matter, each individual must assess personal needs, and plan a way of life that is in harmony with one's temperament. It may appear to be difficult to begin with, but gradually one's thoughts turn into habits, and one lives effortlessly. Each one of us is the architect of our health. We may make it or mar it.

Points to ponder...

- ❑ It is natural to be anxious about one's health.
- ❑ Good health depends upon individual habits and attitudes.
- ❑ To be healthy, understand yourself.
- ❑ You are what you eat.
- ❑ To be physically healthy, one must be emotionally healthy.
- ❑ We are architects of our health. We must have a plan for living.

❖❖

8

Planning a Career

"The best careers advice given to the young is, 'Find out what you like doing best and get someone to pay you for doing it.'"

—Katherine Whitehorn

Almost one-third of one's adult life is spent in pursuing a career. With changing times, women are no less zealous about it than men. Even if they do not pursue a career in the strict sense of the word, their role as a housewife is no less important. It complements the efforts of the husband in achieving success in his career.

Life is becoming more competitive each day, and so is pursuit of a career. Unfortunately, most young people believe that all they need to do is collect diplomas and degrees, and as they come of age, they will find an easy way to a career of their choice. However, experience has shown how wrong they can be. A successful career is not a matter of chance, or sheer luck, as many tend to believe. It depends upon correct planning and foresight.

The Need to Work

Everybody needs to work. It is not only a means to earn money to support oneself, the family, or to promote oneself in society.

It is a medium of expression of one's individuality in life. With the rise in one's career, there is growth of the mental faculties. Work keeps one busy, and makes the mind active and progressive. If one were to remain idle, the devil within soon surfaces, and before long, the charm of living is lost.

A career is as important to women as it is to men. It is often argued that God has ordained all women to be mothers and housewives, and most women seem to agree. However, we should not overlook the fact that housekeeping is as vital as any other career can be. The home is the most important primary institution. It is not only a medium for the expression of womanhood, but a sanctuary for the man who has to tackle the hardships of working in a competitive world. For children, it is a training ground to learn human values. Even otherwise, with increasing needs and a common desire for a higher standard of living, many women are combining their role as a housewife with a full-time career.

Career Opportunities

Most young people complain that sufficient opportunities are not there for a good career. The truth is that they need to understand the situation better. In the first place, what does the word 'opportunity' mean to them? Is it a mysterious force that comes knocking at the doors of a blessed few? Or, is it the power to push and pull in life through recommendations of friends and relatives? To some, it may mean a tailor-made job, or a business handed down by the family. If an opportunity is one of these things, or something similar, then we must admit that opportunities are becoming scarce. But this is not true. An opportunity is no more than a fragment of a thought that conjures up a dream in our mind. Through hard work, we turn this dream into reality.

Job opportunities are not becoming scarce. Each day as new discoveries and inventions are made, or newer services offered, there opens a wide horizon of more opportunities and jobs. In reality, opportunities for good careers continue to grow. The only problem is that competition is also growing. What is worse is that the youth have not been trained to recognise opportunities.

Those who have achieved success did not wait for opportunities to come knocking at their doors. Instead, they created them. The active ingredient of a career is satisfying human wants. It may entail individual action, or group participation, but the financial reward comes in return for the human needs that are being satisfied. Fortunately, since human needs continue to grow, and can really be unlimited, the opportunities also keep growing. To make the most of them, learn to recognise them, and put them to good use.

Selecting a Career

It is unfortunate to note the high percentage of young people who are uncertain of what they would like to do after completing their formal education. Even those who have some idea about a career, know about it only vaguely. Even then their knowledge is based upon the money and the glamour attached to it rather than the capabilities required, or the responsibilities involved, in pursuing it successfully.

The need for an early selection of a suitable career can hardly be overemphasised. Most careers require specialised training. The earlier one gets on the right track, the better it is. A mistake can often prove to be rather expensive. However, since youngsters cannot have a precise idea of the responsibilities and the rewards that go with different careers, the only sensible solution lies in availing of vocational guidance services.

Parents are the best guides for a young person. One cannot doubt their intentions, but most parents are not in a position to guide their children in selecting a career. They can be the best judges of what their children like, or what they do not. Very often they are biased in their opinion of certain careers, and are invariably ignorant of the problems affecting careers other than the one they may pursue.

Many colleges and universities have started vocational guidance services. Students can avail of them for their personal benefit.

Newspapers and magazines are a good source of information on different careers. A library is also a good source of details about careers or about colleges and universities offering courses leading to a career.

The Best Career

Which is the best career one can take up? This question continues to perturb all young people for a long time. The choice is always very difficult to make. Many careers are particularly attractive as there is a lot of glamour or money attached to them. Most young people would opt for them because they only see the brighter aspect, and overlook the simple fact that one needs to give much in return for the glamour and money one expects. In these careers, only the capable and deserving ones achieve success. Even then, the period of success is not very long. The percentage of failures is rather high.

The truth is that all careers are good. They are important and necessary to enable an organised society to run efficiently. However, not everyone is suited for all types of careers. The requirements of each career are variable, demanding different levels of education, competence and ability. The selection would therefore necessarily depend upon individual aptitudes and capabilities. That career can be termed best when a person can put in his best efforts, and finds pleasure not in the money received for the work, but in the satisfaction that comes from doing the job efficiently. The understanding of this truth can save a lot of heartbreaks later.

Self-analysis for Career Selection

Before you can finalise a career you have in mind, it is necessary that you analyse your personal aptitudes, preferences, strong points and weaknesses. Nobody can do this job better than you can. Only you understand both, your personal hopes and aspirations, and your weaknesses. You need to be ruthlessly realistic with yourself. How do you rate your capabilities? Is your education adequate? Do you have any personal shortcomings? If so, can you overcome them? How, and by when? Are your personal capabilities in parity with the needs of the career? Are you mentally well prepared to meet the challenges that it may offer? Many young people over-rate themselves, and feel sorry about it later. Therefore, be modest about your estimates. Answer these questions, and many more as they come to your mind. Write down the answers in a notebook. As you put everything in black and white, you will begin to get a realistic picture of yourself as related to the career you want to take up.

How does this picture compare with that of another person known to you who is already pursuing this particular career? Keeping in view certain variations that are natural, the two pictures should be reasonably identical. Yours should rather be on the brighter side. This way you can be certain that with time you will be able to adapt yourself to the needs of the career, and face the challenges it offers boldly.

Preparing Yourself

Once you have finalised what you would like to do, and ascertained that you have the requisite capabilities to pursue the career, it becomes necessary that you prepare yourself for various challenges it will offer from time to time. It is true that high educational qualifications alone are not enough to ensure success in a career, but we cannot overlook the need for maximum knowledge on the subject. If you are not already equipped with it, you can gain it through specialised training. Postal courses and short-term courses are often very useful in achieving this aim. Even after one has gained a certain amount of workable knowledge, one must continue to improve upon it regularly.

Looking for a Job

After a person is ready to launch himself in a particular career begins the most difficult part in the whole process—the search for a good job. Good jobs are not easy to come by, particularly for those who are just beginning in life. Most employers desire not only the basic qualifications for the job, but also some working experience. Furthermore, few employers have the patience to provide the initial on-the-job training that is necessary to work efficiently. However, the situation is not as bad as it often appears to be. One does keep coming across job opportunities, and one needs to keep one's eyes and ears open to grab the right position.

It is useful to get oneself registered with a placement agency. They will get in touch with you whenever an opening exists. Many newspapers and magazines regularly display advertisements about job vacancies in both the classified and the display sections. Government departments also advertise in the national and local newspapers depending upon the type of vacancy. For those who have a specialised career in mind, it is best to look through advertisements in trade journals. It is not practical for a person looking for a job to simultaneously subscribe to the many newspapers and magazines that carry the 'positions vacant' advertisements. The best solution lies in going through these publications at the local library.

For those interested in highly specialised lines, or when it is known that the number of employers who could be interested in their services is limited, it would be useful to write directly to the personnel departments of prospective employers informing them about the availability of one's services. Even if a position is not immediately vacant, it is customary for employers to keep such applications filed so that they may refer to it whenever an opening occurs. Many such applications have resulted in worthwhile jobs.

Understanding Job Requirements

When you come across an advertisement offering a job which you think you can fill, do not hasten to send an application by the first post. Read the advertisement carefully repeatedly. Try to read between the lines. Out of necessity, most advertisements need to be short and to the point. To avoid unnecessary effort, expense, or heartbreak later, one needs to understand the exact requirements of the advertiser.

After reading the advertisement, ask yourself: What are the job requirements? Has the advertiser placed any restrictions on the age of the applicants? What qualifications does he desire? What is the salary offered? Where would you be expected to work? Does the job require you to shift residence, or break the present family bonds? Are there any problems about securing proper residential accommodation in the area of your work? One needs to consider these important issues. Your securing the job, and making a success of it, depends upon them. If you cannot fulfil the basic requirements of the job, or know that you will not be able to adjust your family life to give your job the best of yourself, it is best to forget about it right away.

However, if you feel confident that you understand the needs of the advertiser, and can provide them efficiently and conveniently, go ahead and apply for the job. While it is essential that the employer must get the best you can offer, it is equally important that you must get the satisfaction of doing your job well. Mutual benefit is the basis of all good employer-employee relationships.

The Best Employer

There are several factors like working conditions, pay scales, security of service, fringe benefits, bonus, etc., on the basis of which employers can be classified. Since it is natural for everyone to desire to work for an employer who offers the maximum security of service, many young people prefer government jobs. Of course, these jobs too have their own good and bad points. Therefore, one must weigh them in keeping with individual preferences. Many times, no choices are possible. Whenever possible, it is advisable that a young person taking up his first job opt for a position that helps him gain on-the-job experience. This makes it possible for him to rise steadily in his career. The smaller companies often offer this advantage. There one is likely to handle more responsibility, and be in a position to try new ideas. One can learn a lot in these jobs. Unfortunately, the salaries offered are less as compared to larger concerns. As one gains experience and confidence to handle responsibility, the remuneration increases. Where such ability is important, both the larger and the smaller companies offer similar wage scales. Very highly paid jobs are offered only by larger concerns. Such jobs require a high degree of experience, which is not within the reach of a young person just embarking upon a career.

Applying for the Job

Once you are mentally convinced that the job advertised is just the right one for you, draft an application. Since employers like to interview all the worthwhile candidates before they issue a letter of employment, it is obvious that there will be many dropouts at this stage. Therefore, an important purpose that your communication must fulfil is to get you an interview call. To ensure this, your application must be a fair representation of your qualifications and abilities as required for the job.

At this stage, you will do well to remember that the employer has offered an opening because it will enable him to further his own interests. His interests in the job are limited to the gains he can get out of it. If you wish to secure your own interests, you will need to watch the interests of your employer.

In your application, mention the details of your academic career, special extra-curricular interests and achievements, jobs held, if any. Support information regarding qualifications, and special achievements, with copies of your certificates. Originals should not be sent. These can be shown at the time of the interview. If references are required, then you can draw upon the good relations you enjoy with your family doctor, or some of your father's friends. Be as brief as possible. The purpose of the application is to give the prospective employer a fair idea of your personal capabilities.

From the rough draft prepare the final application. Check the facts, the spellings etc. Finally, using good quality paper, type it neatly. If you have a personal letterhead, you can use it. A plain white paper of good quality can serve the purpose. It would be in order to send a handwritten application, if you have a neat handwriting. Make certain that it is clear and legible. Keep a copy of the application for your record.

Some employers may require the application be made on a prescribed form that they may supply on request, or on payment. In that case, write down the details required in rough on a separate sheet, and finally fill them neatly and legibly on the form, avoiding any overwriting. Keep a copy of the information provided for your record.

Preparing for the Interview

If your application meets the requirements of the job advertised, the chances are that you will get an interview call. Begin preparing for the interview, which will be an important meeting. To understand the needs of your prospective employer better, find out all you can about the company—its set-up, branches, its products and services. If you can, then also find out all about the responsibilities and privileges of the position for which you have applied. Such information can be collected from advertisements in the national press, advertisement literature, house journals, the local distributors, and even the local retailers. Information about other companies in a similar trade can also prove useful. Thus equipped, you will be in a better position to answer important questions at the interview.

When you receive a call, immediately acknowledge it, confirming the place, day and time mentioned in the letter. Have your file containing the original documents mentioned in your application ready. Although it is natural for ambitious young people to search for better positions, many employers do not like it. Therefore, if you are already employed somewhere, you need not mention it as a reason for desiring leave. Ask for leave to attend to certain personal matters.

The Purpose of the Interview

The purpose of an interview is to afford an opportunity to the prospective employer to gauge the personal capabilities of the candidates who have applied for the position.

During the interview, the employer would like to confirm the facts you may have mentioned in your application. He will also want to gauge your knowledge, special interests and achievements, the ability to learn new skills and your willingness to work under given circumstances. The ability to make decisions is vital to many jobs, and he may want to judge your ability in this direction also. The interview will afford him an occasion to assess your general image. Employers are particularly interested in the health and personality as exhibited by one's poise, manners and sense of dress. He may also want to know about past successes and failures, and how you faced them. Your reactions and answers to the interviewer's questions will help him conclude to what extent you are suitable.

The Interview

Be appropriately dressed. Make certain you are well groomed. The original certificates and documents must be carried in a neat file.

When you arrive for the interview, do not try to get friendly with the receptionist, or the other candidates, and start comparing notes and qualifications. Do not overlook the simple fact that they are your competitors. Avoid unnecessary tension. Do not smoke either. You can profitably spend your time until you are called by reading a newspaper, or a book. If you prefer to read a book, then do not read cheap fiction.

Your prospective employer may be reading it also, but when it comes to employees, most employers desire that they should read constructive books.

When you are called in, remember that a good first impression is important. Take a deep breath, and enter with a smile. This helps in doing away with nervousness. Sit down when asked to. Let the interviewer start the conversation. He will want to hear you rather than speak himself, but never interrupt the interviewer. Hear him carefully, and answer clearly and audibly. Do not use slang, or smoke even if the interviewer offers you a cigarette. If you have mentioned some special interests and achievements in your application, the interviewer may want to know more about them. Answer the questions in simple language to convey the correct meaning. Do not forget that your power of expression is on test.

The interviewer may want to test your reactions in special circumstances, and may therefore ask provocative questions, or broach controversial subjects. Such occasions demand tact and patience. Do not be provoked under any circumstances. Be cool, and discuss your viewpoint with a smile.

If you are changing jobs, explain that reasonably too. Do not blame those with whom you work presently. It would be more acceptable if you were to say that the circumstances do not suit you, rather than that your present employer has made things difficult for you. If your interviewer asks you about a subject you don't know anything about, do not be afraid to confess your ignorance. If it is something vital you do not know about, you can still express your ignorance, and apologise for it. Your sincerity will be appreciated.

Interviewers are ordinary people, and may have their whims and fancies. At the same time, they have an eye for people with ability. They will not immediately disclose whether you have been selected, but before concluding the interview he may ask you if you want to know anything in particular. You can avail of this opportunity to clarify doubts, if any, about the prospects of the job, the fringe benefits, etc. but be extremely brief and specific.

Intelligence Tests

Besides the interview, many employers prefer to give candidates an intelligence test to ascertain their IQ, or grade them according to certain specifications. The results of these tests are certainly not conclusive. Different employers place varying degrees of importance on the results. These tests aim at gauging one's mental agility, power of reasoning, comprehension, memory, etc., and are invariably short, require little writing, and must be answered in a limited period.

The important thing is to avoid tension. Before undergoing the test, read the instructions carefully. Go through the test answering the questions that you can. Do not get anxious if you cannot answer a question. Leave it, and move on to the next one. This way you can go through the test answering all the questions which you can, and return to the difficult ones later if time permits, as you would in your school or college exams.

The IQ of a person depends upon various factors like family background, education, age, residence, personal problems, the weather, mood, and even the town from where one comes. Women have been found to be as intelligent as men, but they have lesser interests than men. People who score well in these tests are those who spend time in self-improvement regularly.

Negotiating a Salary

While advertising a job most employers specify the salary and the scale of pay offered but sometimes the matter is open to negotiation. Though the employer knows what salary the job carries, he wants to test the candidate, and find out his aspirations and stage of development.

If you are already employed and changing jobs, you can relate the expected salary to what you are already receiving. However, if this is your first job, you must make reliable enquiries, and find out what the job is worth. This can be done by studying advertisements for similar jobs, or through people already in similar positions. Demand a salary accordingly. Never show a lack of decision in these matters. If the employer finds you worthy of the amount, he will pay it. If you are capable, and the difference is nominal, he will explain his stand to you.

Changing Jobs

Generally, the first job may not be the one that offers the maximum opportunity for growth and progress. Employers consider those who change jobs too often as unstable. When an opportunity does arise, study it thoroughly before taking it up. Consider both the advantages and disadvantages of changing the job. Many times the increase in fringe benefits may only be illusory. To justify a change of jobs, there should be an increase in salary, more responsibility, better chances of promotion, and lots of job satisfaction. Then only would a change be worthwhile.

Points to ponder...

- ❑ Everybody needs to work to support oneself and the family.
- ❑ Select a career that is in harmony with your personality.
- ❑ Prepare yourself for the career through good education.
- ❑ Understand job requirements. Prepare to fulfil them.
- ❑ Look for employment opportunities where you can learn and grow.
- ❑ Always put in your best efforts.

❖❖

9

Recreation

"He that will make a good use of any part of his life must allow a large part of it to recreation."

—Locke

Recreation is as important as work in everyday life. A certain amount of tension continues to build within everyone all the time. This is irrespective of the fact whether one is physically or mentally occupied. Recreation gives a vent to this tension. If this tension does not find a suitable outlet, it gradually builds up to cause an excessive pressure on some part of the body. Eventually, this pressure finds an outlet in the shape of an illness.

Recreation can mean many things—a diversion in the normal activities, taking part in some form of play, or it may refer to the simple pleasure of physical relaxation. Besides helping to release the tension of everyday life, recreation is useful in being mentally and physically stimulating. This naturally leads one to greater achievement. However, one is liable to misunderstand the importance of recreation. One may misplace priorities, thereby forsaking the many advantages that accrue from it. It is therefore imperative that one should understand how recreation affects us in everyday life.

Recreation in Everyday Life

Since recreation breaks the monotony of everyday life by offering a change from the ordinary, one finds it pleasant. Many people associate everything pleasant as being dirty, sinful and corrupting. At best, these people feel that recreation is only for those who can afford the luxuries of life. This is not true. Whatever we may feel about this vital subject, the truth is that not only is recreation important as a part of the daily routine, but also that each one of us does have one way or another of personal recreation.

Some forms of recreation entail physical activity. Others do not. Each form has its own advantages and shortcomings, but all serve the purpose. Recreation should rightly form a part of daily life. It helps to free onself from the grip of tension. It promotes creative living. Even nature desires it that way. It gives us compulsory rest each day through sleep.

Let us consider some of the usual methods of recreation adopted by most young people to suit their individual liking.

Outdoor Activities

Outdoor activities like athletics, swimming, gymnastics and games like football, hockey and cricket offer an excellent form of recreation. These provide not only a change from the ordinary, but also provide useful exercise for the maintenance of good health. Through an interest in these activities, young people can channelise the bountiful energy nature provides them during adolescence in a constructive way. Such activities inculcate a spirit of discipline, the need for cooperative action, and a desire to be fair to all concerned. It is because of these overwhelming advantages that such activities are encouraged in schools and colleges all over.

Since proficiency in these activities is an asset in adult life, many prospective employers take it as an added qualification when a person has done well in these activities during his school and college life. Where huge playing grounds are not available, young people can take an active interest in outdoor games like badminton, volley-ball, lawn tennis, etc. and indoor games like table tennis, chess etc. Activities like trekking and mountaineering provide wonderful experiences.

Recreation Indoors

Indoor recreation facilities that can keep young people busy usefully during their leisure are almost unlimited in scope. Much depends upon individual choice and attitude as to what interests a person. Some like to spend their time playing indoor games like carrom and chess. Others may like to cultivate a hobby, visit a library, or read something for pleasure at home. Some may spend the time peacefully hearing favourite tunes on the radio, a music system, or perhaps watching television. All these activities provide a welcome change from the regular routine, and are often mentally stimulating. However, most of these activities offer food only for the mind. They offer almost no exercise. There is another disadvantage in that one may indulge in these activities crossing the limits for reasonable recreation. This may in the end be a problem rather than an asset.

Cultivating a Hobby

A hobby can be a great source of creative stimulation. It can keep one busy for long periods, and can often promote friendship with people sharing similar interests. Some hobbies are purely recreative, but others can be useful in the home. Some can even help one to earn a few extra rupees. Hobbies can also be useful in understanding one's needs and preferences, and later, in the selection of a suitable career.

It is difficult to tell as to which is the best hobby one can take up. The ultimate selection of a hobby depends upon individual needs and aptitudes. It is important that the hobby must be interesting, and one should find pleasure in it. It is also important that one should not spend too much money on a hobby initially as it may fail to hold a person's interest for long. The hobby must be developed gradually as one finds the effort and the expense on it worthwhile. Sharing a hobby with friends can be useful to develop it, and to provide mental stimulation.

Social Gatherings

One always enjoys the company of friends. It is both relaxing and stimulating. Some people develop friendships easily, others do not. Some like to develop a wide circle of friends. However, most people are satisfied with only a few friends. Much depends upon individual attitudes, upon one's expectations and outlook about such relationships. Since human beings are gregarious by nature, one finds these relationships satisfying. There is a natural release of tension when people talk to each other.

Friendships develop from sharing mutual interests. One's company has a profound effect upon one's thoughts, actions and habits, and one tends to accept the easy ways of life more readily. Therefore, one needs to be careful about friends who may lead one away from established values. One also needs to be aware about the need for a certain form of etiquette to make relationships with friends congenial. A feeling of mutual give-and-take promotes goodwill amongst friends.

Smoking and Drinking

A common outcome of group get-togethers is experimentation with smoking and drinking. With growing independence and freedom from parental supervision, smoking and drinking amongst young people is on the rise. Most young people make a beginning just to be loyal to their group, but some want to taste the unknown. It is not long before one may begin to like it, and eventually accept this as a means of recreation in everyday life.

Both smoking and drinking are temporarily relaxing. One often mistakes this relaxation to be real, but it is not so. The effect is deceptive. Besides being an expensive habit, smoking increases the incidence of heart disease and lung cancer. The use of alcohol makes one a potential risk on the road. It affects one's sense of time and space. Continued use of alcohol can also damage the vital organs in the body. It would be best if young people avoid these vices.

The Truth About Drugs

The use of drugs to promote a feeling of relaxation is not new. With rapid technological advances in modern medicine, there are many new drugs. Their widespread use by doctors to relieve tension and stress symptoms has made many people aware of the rapid relief these can provide. They are, therefore, tempted to try them more freely as a means of promoting a feeling of relaxation and rest.

Drugs can affect individuals in many ways. Some drugs are stimulating and produce a feeling of well-being. Others give pleasure through elimination of symptoms of anxiety, stress and fatigue, and promote restful sleep. Another kind has a fascinating effect in producing fantasies, which are a unique experience each time. Apparently, there appears to be no harm in the use of drugs to promote relaxation. However, the truth is that the research work done on these drugs is so meagre that their complete effect on individuals is not fully understood. While some people do benefit temporarily from their use, there have been cases of psychotic shock in others even when administered in minute quantities. The feelings of confidence and creativity which some drugs are said to produce are not real. Use of drugs by young people should be totally avoided except under expert medical attention.

Recreational Sex

The expression of sexual desire is accompanied by intense pleasure. It promotes release of tension, a feeling of relaxation, and a desire for sleep. Human beings are capable of having sexual relations anytime, even without the need of procreation. Therefore, with the awakening of sexual desire during adolescence, the recreational aspect of sex begins to draw the attention of young people.

Since society places certain restraints upon the normal expression of sexual desire by young people until they are emotionally prepared to shoulder the responsibility of looking after a family, the initial experiences may be through masturbation. Some may also experiment with a homosexual relationship, or with a willing partner of the opposite sex. Since these experiences are necessarily secret, they are accompanied by a guilt complex. By all standards, they are incomplete, and offer no more than a physical outlet. A wholesome expression of sexual desire comes only gradually with a willing partner through marriage.

Balanced Recreation

The ultimate aim of every progressive person should be to create a fair balance between work and recreation in everyday life. No single form of recreation can be complete. Needs change with time. One often combines more than one form of recreation to fill the vacant moments of life. This provides rest, and is mentally stimulating. Tensions must be got rid of from time to time. Intermingle rest and work. Do not economise on sleep. Try to understand your personal needs, and adopt ways whereby you can always perform at your very best.

Points to ponder...

- ❑ Recreation is as important as work in everyday life.
- ❑ Assess your own recreational needs.
- ❑ Games promote creativity, good health and well-being.
- ❑ Understand the dangers of smoking, drinking and drugs.
- ❑ Create a fair balance between work and recreation.

10

The Art of Successful Living

"The man who succeeds above his fellows is the one who, early in life, clearly discerns his object, and towards that object habitually directs his powers. Even genius itself is but fine observation strengthened by fixity of purpose. Every man who observes vigilantly and resolves steadfastly grows unconsciously into genius."

—Bulwer

It is natural for everyone to desire successful living. People are judged by the sum total of success they achieve in various spheres of life. These often reflect their personal income, position and status in society. It is the smaller achievement in day-to-day living which accumulate into bigger achievements, and make a person stand out in a crowd.

Successful living is not a matter of chance. Luck or the hidden fortunes of nature do play a vital part. However, their influence is more of degree than of kind. The real success comes from consciously, or subconsciously, making a deliberate effort in the right direction. Certain factors affect successful living. One needs to understand these, and make them work in everyday life. That way everyone can make successful living a constant companion.

What is Success?

What does success mean to you? Lots of money? A home of your own? A small fortune set aside? A happy family? Fame and popularity? It could mean one of these things, or perhaps something quite different. Success does mean different things to everyone. Each one of us pursues it in our own individual way. To live successfully means to be able to realise personal ambition. The way of achieving success has to be in harmony with an individual's personality. The basic factors affecting successful living operate in the same manner in all cases.

A Slow Process

At the outset, every young person must remember that climbing the ladder of success is a slow process. One must go up step by step. There is no shortcut. Many young people are tempted by the desire for quick gains. They search for ways and means whereby their aim is quickly realised. Invariably such attempts are futile. Sometimes, one does achieve a certain amount of success quickly. However, if one is not personally capable and hard working, the success can only be temporary. In such cases, with time, one slips back to the level where he belongs. One can only maintain those heights that are in parity with personal capabilities. Personal capabilities are related directly to one's knowledge and experience. Both of these are gained gradually through steady effort. One learns to live successfully through trial and error, and by avoiding the past mistakes. This way success comes slowly, but surely.

The Right Age

Many young people are guilty of waiting for success to come into their lives with time. They feel that when they come to a certain age, they will automatically begin to live a successful life. However, it is not so. One does not need to wait for success. One must pursue it. If one can understand various factors that affect personal success, and can use them in everyday life, there is no reason why one cannot live successfully. Personal desires in childhood are different from those in adult life. The type of desires do not reflect personal success. It is the extent to which one can fulfil personal desires that reflects one's ability to live successfully. Some learn to make the factors affecting success to work for them at an early age. There are others who may learn to do so in their twenties, thirties, or even later. Age does not attract success. Knowledge and experience do. Those who learn it early, make it a life-long companion.

Level of Personal Ability

One infallible law of nature is that a person achieves and maintains success in proportion to his personal ability. The hidden hand of destiny does play its part. However, nothing can be achieved if one lacks personal capabilities, and only hopes for luck to take one towards a particular goal. Those who have definite targets to achieve cannot wait forever for luck to strike. If they must reach their destination, they must cover a certain distance on the path to success day after day. Setting targets means nothing unless there is a deadline by which they must be achieved.

Success comes from putting in every bit of one's personal ability into whatever a person undertakes to do. The more capable you are, the better the chances of success. If you lack knowledge, take steps to make it a part of you. If you do not keep good health, see what adjustments you need to make so that it may not hinder you from achieving your goal. Learn to observe and adapt other people's ideas, their mode of working, and their success. From this one gains vital experience—a valuable ingredient of personal ability. Increasing personal ability is decidedly a slow process. Once a person has made it a part of himself, it remains with him for life, winning success in various spheres of life.

Stepping Stones to Success

Every successful person follows a set pattern to achieve success. The foundation of success is built by defining definite goals in life. Unless one knows where he wants to go, he cannot hope to reach his destination. For convenience, these goals can be broken up into smaller targets. They may be revised as one gets along in life, but it is important that goals must be realistic, and in parity with the personal capabilities of the person who desires to achieve them.

Once the goals are in clear sight, the next step is to formulate a plan to achieve them. In preparing the plans, use your imagination. If you have your convictions to back you, do not be afraid to be different. Men and women who dared to be different have brought about all progress. Through action, they proved that they were right.

Finally, success comes from putting the plans into action. Nothing can be achieved unless one works for it. Working regularly with a spirit of dedication is a factor that contributes the most towards successful living. There is no alternative to work. What needs to be done, must be done. One must concentrate on what one sets out to do, putting in every bit of energy that is available. This way, one reaches the destination sooner. Most of the obstacles one comes across in pursuit of success show up as one works for it. We will discuss some of the important aspects of the problem in the paragraphs that follow.

The Dignity of Labour

One important factor which is holding up millions of young people from achieving success is their hesitation to look at all vocations as being honourable and necessary to an organised society. Unfortunately, these young people look down at manual labour. Only white-collar jobs attract them although they offer no prospects for progress. These people do not use their academic achievements for personal growth. They use these to differentiate themselves from the active working classes. Having achieved a certain academic level, these young people feel that it is below their dignity to do manual work. Although most young people aspire for high executive positions, and for jobs which have a lot of glamour and show attached to them, little do they realise that very few people have the ability to reach very high positions. Those who have reached there had to start at the bottom of the ladder. Behind their rise are many years of hard work and toil backed by personal ability.

Any work that fulfils a need of society is both dignified and worthwhile. For people who aim high, no work should be too big, or too small. Education aims at making a person more competent to tackle different kinds of work.

Do Not be Easily Satisfied

Another valuable secret of living successfully is never to be easily satisfied with one's performance. One must constantly aim to do better each time. It does not matter whether it is at home or at work or whether you are self-employed or working for someone; it is essential that your productivity gradually rise. When you offer a little more than what is expected of you, you are indirectly making it evident that you are capable of handling more responsibility than what you are presently doing. As one learns to give more service and handle increased responsibility, one gradually moves up until one can fully handle the responsibility involved in a higher position. The habit of giving more service than expected always wins many grateful clients and customers who ultimately contribute towards one's success.

Try New Ideas

Many people have learnt to live successfully through their willingness to try out new ideas. If it were not for the daring of such people, perhaps no progress would have been possible in any sphere of life. It is this minority who venture into the unknown by backing their ideas with action, and are rewarded with success. Each day, many new products are marketed, and special services offered. Behind each one of them is the spirit of adventure, the desire to turn a dream into reality. Of course, not all ideas work out successfully. Nevertheless, most of the ideas that have been well considered do work out, and rightly attract the rewards of material benefits and recognition, both of which are signs of success.

A certain amount of success comes from being different from the rest. This does not mean that one must be different just for the sake of being different. One should take to the unknown path only when one is satisfied that the odds are in one's favour, when one has the ability and confidence to prove that the idea is feasible. Those who wish to be successful should be fearless. To ensure success, come out with new ideas, and then show everyone that you can make them work.

Avoid Procrastination

One habit that is holding back innumerable young people from achieving success is their habit of procrastination. Many people have the right kind of ideas, and are willing to back them with work. However, when they put off until tomorrow what they should really be doing today, it is not surprising that success eludes them. It is important that action is taken at the right time. Time plays as significant a role in successful living as any other factor.

One field in which most people come into the clutches of procrastination is that of decision making. Rather than make a decision, most people wish that things would sort out on their own. Can we expect such people to be successful? In decision making there are fifty percent chances that you would be right, but when one becomes indecisive, you can be certain that you will always be wrong.

Motivating Yourself

Successful people do not wait for moments of inspiration to stimulate them to reach greater heights, but constantly motivate themselves to perform well all the time. Their secret lies in having learnt what form of stimulus they respond to favourably. Thereafter, whenever they find their performance falling, they recharge themselves with their favourite source of creative stimulation, and continue to perform well.

Different people respond differently to various forms of mental stimulation. In each case, the response of a person to a particular form of stimulation is the same. Some are inspired to perform better by hearing their favourite music, others by praise, and there are still others who may prefer a quiet evening in the garden, or by the fireside. The means of stimulation can be as varied as people can be. It does not matter what inspires you. Once you know what it is, keep yourself fully charged. Build around you an environment that inspires you to reach your goal. Keep reminding yourself of the many rewards of success, and as you turn your full capabilities into action, you soon find out how easy it is to live successfully.

Enjoy Your Work

All successful people enjoy doing whatever they take up. It does not matter whether they are doing an insignificant task, or handling some vital responsibility; they accept both with grace and pleasure. One can immediately notice the stability, tranquillity and efficiency in everything they do. Contrary to this, the average person grumbles about everything he needs to do. He will grumble about his family, about his boss, his colleagues and everything else. To him each day is no more than another day "at the grind".

Everybody needs to put in a certain amount of work in return for the benefits one desires and derives from society. One can do it happily, or grudgingly. The difference lies in the individual attitude. When one enjoys doing his assignments, they can be completed quickly and efficiently, leaving time for leisure. On the other hand, if one only grumbles about it, the work will appear more difficult, and may remain undone. Look forward to your day as another opportunity to live successfully and to move on to your goals in life.

Honesty and Integrity

Many young people look for shortcuts to material success, and are lured by easy gains through dishonest means. Such people cannot be said to be successful in the real sense. They only pretend to be successful by showing off the material benefits they have so gained. Such gains are temporary, and in the end, one has to pay for them many times more by the loss of personal values.

The greatest source of strength to all successful people is their character, which in turn depends upon personal values of the individual concerned. Honesty and integrity are of particular significance in everyday life. It is true that the path of honesty and integrity is very difficult. But life built upon them is always full of achievements.

Dealing with People

The people around us accept us either as being successful or otherwise. To them each one of us is what they think we are. Therefore, the image we project of ourselves is very important. One's personality, poise, manners, clothes, and most important of all, concern for others, are factors which affect our personal image in society. Whether this image is projected well, or in a distorted manner, is important.

Many young people assert that they do not care for what others think of them. This may be all right to a certain degree. Nobody can please everyone. We cannot overlook that in everyday life we need to deal with lots of people. Unless we can be successful in our dealings with them, we cannot be accepted as successful. At home there are our parents, brothers, sisters and other relatives; in professional life, there are subordinates, colleagues and seniors. We need to gain their approval.

So difficult is the art of dealing with people that those who have learnt the secrets of this art are the highest paid and most respected people in the world. The secret of being successful with people lies in accepting them as they are, and not as you would like them to be. To each individual, his hopes and aspirations are important. He wants them to be honoured and respected. You do not need to lose your own individuality. When you respect others' sentiments and feelings, and are thoughtful towards them, you automatically help generate goodwill, and become successful in dealing with people.

Handling Criticism

A common virtue of all successful people is the intelligent handling of criticism that is levelled against them. Criticism is very much like the force of gravity. The higher you are on the ladder of success, the more it pulls you down. It can often assume nagging proportions. If one does not learn how to handle it patiently and tactfully, it is not long before a person gets discouraged, and falls off the ladder of success. Courageous people use criticism to their advantage, rather than as an obstacle.

One fact is very clear. When a person is criticised, he is surely on his way to success. Criticism always comes from people who lack enthusiasm and perseverance to become successful themselves. Intelligent people on their way up do not let criticism deter them from their goals. Instead, they use it as a guide to plug in any loopholes they may have overlooked in the course of their efforts.

Facing Obstacles

The road to successful living is loaded with obstacles almost at every step. Until one is well armed with experience, there might be many occasions when a person has to face defeat. This could be due to miscalculations of various descriptions or due to human failures, and sometimes due to natural limitations. However, what one needs to understand is that these defeats are common to all who are in search of success, and that these are temporary. It is true that most young people are overwhelmed with these obstacles. They prefer to give up the struggle to live a simpler, uneventful and insignificant life.

However, no person in the pursuit of successful living can achieve his goal unless he perseveres. It is indeed unfortunate that though endowed with natural enthusiasm, most young people give up only a few steps away from their goal. If they could only keep up their efforts for a little more time, they would have made it to their destination.

The secret lies in not letting the obstacles frighten you. Keep going even when others have fallen out. Keep motivating yourself by repeating in your mind that success is just around the corner. Think of the many rewards of success that await you. Think of the recognition it will endow upon you. The more enthusiastic you feel, the lesser will be the chances of your getting easily discouraged. Anticipate obstacles. Be prepared to face them when they come. This way you will ensure your continued success.

Self-improvement

We live in a highly competitive world. It is not enough to reach a certain stature in life. To be accepted as a successful person, it is important that one must be able to maintain the level of one's achievements day after day. This is by no means an easy task. All around us, knowledge is rapidly growing, and so competition is becoming stiffer. If a person does not want to be left behind in life, it is necessary that one regularly devote some time for self-improvement. All successful people have made it a part of their everyday life. So can you. Read books and magazines that pertain to your business or professional life. Read on subjects that affect your health, happiness and prosperity. You could also take up refresher courses, correspondence courses, or join a club where you can meet people who share your interests. The important thing is that you must continue to widen the horizon of your interests, and you will add on to your achievements. Successful living aims at gradually building the individual, and as you go on accumulating smaller successes, they will add the power to achieve greater success in life.

Points to ponder...

- ❑ Success comes to those who know how to succeed.
- ❑ Success comes slowly.
- ❑ Prepare yourself for success everyday.
- ❑ No work is too small to be done. No problem is too big to resolve.
- ❑ Learn to motivate yourself.
- ❑ Enjoy whatever you do.

❖❖

11

Falling in Love

"Love is a thing to be learned. It is difficult, complex maintenance of individual integrity throughout the incalculable processes of inter-human polarity."

—D.H. Lawrence

Love is the greatest of all emotions. The dictionary defines it as *a strong liking or interest; an ardent affection or fondness; to caress, fondle, or to take great interest in something*. We all know that nothing could be more pleasurable than to be loved. Whatever it may mean to each one of us, one thing is certain. We need it to keep alive in body and spirit.

There is great power in love. It gives strength to both the lover and the loved. It can be likened to the power of God. It immediately wins human goodwill, can turn enemies into friends, and can bind friendships with bonds that only death can separate. We need love as it works wonders for us. We also need to understand forces that make it work. There are many forms of love. We need to recognise it in its best form. We must also understand what one needs to give to make it enrich our everyday life.

The Changing Needs of Love

We continue to need love throughout life. Only with time and age, the form of love changes. The unborn child has bonds with the mother through the womb. As a baby, the mother's love satisfies it. It is one-sided in that the baby receives and enjoys it, but gives nothing in return except for the pleasure the mother may derive from it. However, as we grow up we begin to understand our relationship with parents, brothers and sisters, and realise that receiving of love is not all. There is pleasure in giving it too. Sharing our blessings with the family and friends, and consideration of others' feelings begin to give us pleasure, satisfaction and happiness.

With the growing contact with father, brothers, sisters and friends, contact with the world outside the home also grows. We begin to experience changing needs in our relationships with others. Gradually we realise the potentialities of love in winning human goodwill that can add to our happiness and personal power. With age, we also become aware of romantic love that stimulates creativity, and eventually leads to the physical and emotional union between a man and a woman. Through it, the foundations of the institution of the home and family are laid, and mankind continues to grow.

Love and the Opposite Sex

During adolescence when young boys and girls begin to grow physically, and come into greater contact with the environment, they become aware of the opposite sex. In the beginning the contact may only be through group meetings as in co-educational schools, at family gatherings, social functions, at clubs, picnics, or at other similar occasions.

These contacts are useful in that they help young people to learn about basic human relationships. With time and experience, the general sphere of contacts increases.

However, with greater understanding of individual likes and dislikes, the area of active interest is likely to narrow down as one is able to sort out individuals who share common interests. At this stage most young people are choosy about developing intense friendships, but the bonds are invariably strong, and many of these last a lifetime. These friendships often provide opportunities to enable one to come closer to individuals of the opposite sex, and through better understanding, mental bonds may grow to turn a friendship into an intimate relationship.

Teenage Crushes

A crush is a term applied to that first infatuation between a very young boy and girl that is often called "puppy love". It also refers to the secret admiration and love a young person may develop for an elder person; one who is very often a popular personality in real life at home, in school or college, or for a national sportsman, a national leader, or a film star.

These crushes are common amongst young boys and girls, and represent only a passing phase in the process of growing up. This is a time when one is gradually separating from the closer influence of parents, and beginning to find friendship, love and appreciation elsewhere.

Dating

Although dating is an accepted part of living in the west, with the increasing number of co-educational institutions and greater freedom for boys and girls in all spheres of life, it is becoming universally popular.

Contrary to what many believe, the primary purpose of dating is not to select a life partner. It also does not aim at providing an opportunity to experiment with the newly acquired sexual desire. Dating is intended to prepare young boys and girls for mature relationships in adult life. It affords them an opportunity to share common interests, find companionship, and to know and accept varying views about life and living.

Dating may lead one to an intimate relationship. With time, this enables a person to evaluate personal needs, and helps in promoting better understanding of basic human relationships that affect adult life.

When to Begin Dating

What is the right age for young people to begin dating? Maturing of a person is an individual process, and we cannot specify a definite age for everyone. Besides, girls grow and mature faster than boys. They are, therefore, ready for dating earlier. However, only when one is 16 years or above, and is able to enjoy the freedom which studying in a college offers, does one begin to date. Depending upon opportunities, and individual feelings and attitudes, there are some who may not date until they are 20 years old, or even later. Whenever young people do begin dating, they find it an exhilarating experience.

Dating Etiquette

All young people spend many anxious moments during their first few dates. The boys worry about their appearance, manners and habits. On the other hand, the girls are anxious about their clothes, and appearance. Both may be tongue-tied, and feel rather awkward and uneasy, but it is not long before they grow out of these anxieties.

Several other problems vex all young people who go dating. Where should they go? Who spends the money? What about conveyance? Should they exchange gifts and presents? How late can they stay away from home? Would it be all right to hold hands, or kiss each other? It is not possible to answer all these questions in rigid terms because of the obvious variations in individual attitudes and preferences. However, one can still follow simple commonsense rules to make dating pleasant and enjoyable.

The problem as to where one should go is not very difficult to resolve. Some may like to go to a nearby park, a garden, or a picnic spot. Others may prefer to go to a movie, or a theatre, or perhaps for dinner at a restaurant. Others may visit a discotheque, or a dance club. Some may prefer to get together at home, and spend an evening sharing common interests like books, stamps, coins, or even listening to their favourite music. All forms of activities are all right, provided both find them enjoyable.

Although many young people can claim to own a means of conveyance, this can pose a difficult problem for those who are not so blessed. Many forms of transportation are available in most towns and cities. Depending upon individual pockets and convenience, one could choose accordingly.

Many young people feel inferior if they do not have conveyance of their own, and many times may go out of the way by hiring a taxi when they really cannot afford it. Under such circumstances, dating can hardly be any fun. So, the best rule is: do not show off. The chances are that the young lady is of the same social and financial background as you are, and both of you should have a fair understanding about such matters. Do not let trifles spoil your fun.

There is often some misunderstanding as to who should be spending on a date. Many girls expect that since they are invited out, it is the duty of the young man to foot the bill. However, most girls are fair about it, and realise that their companion has limited means. Since the basic object of dating is companionship, it is absolutely in order if young people go Dutch, each paying one's share. Occasionally, one could pay for the other.

Exchange of gifts is an issue which individuals can best sort out themselves. Normally, it is not necessary to give a gift unless there is a special occasion. Even then, since giving and receiving gifts is a two-way gesture, it is important that the value of the gift should be such as not to cause undue embarrassment to either person. The value of the gift does not matter. It is the sentiment that counts.

A problem that often bothers parents more than it does young people is that at times the latter stay away from home for longer than what seems fair. With time, they begin to realise it too. Avoid late nights. To play safe, tell your parents with whom you are going out, and where. Also, when they can expect you back. If you are late, you must make it a point to inform your parents about it on the telephone.

Should young dating couples hold hands, kiss, or become unduly intimate? To comprehend this problem, young people would do well to understand that emotionally men and women are very different. Each action may be interpreted differently by each partner. Certain moral standards have been bred into us through customs and conventions. We need to respect these in our own interests. The best thing to do is to observe a certain amount of self-restraint until one is emotionally mature to understand the implications involved. This ensures a fair balance between one's feelings, and what society desires from us. Dating is intended to provide companionship with the opposite sex, and that is all one should look forward to.

Love at First Sight

Sometimes when a young man and woman meet each other for the first time, their very first glance tells them that they are made for each other. They are introduced, and they get down to talk about their common interests. As though some mysterious force was working, all barriers between the two fade away. This is what is often referred to as love at first sight.

Can this form of instant love hold a couple together in an adult mature relationship? Young people often search for an answer to this question. It is doubtful if such feelings are based upon sufficient reasoning, and can stand the test of time. What a young couple consider to be love may really be no more than a simple attraction towards each other. The newly awakened desire to be independent of the existing family bonds tempts young people to place their confidence elsewhere. With the simultaneous awareness of the opposite sex, it is not surprising that a couple may confess love at first sight. In a mature adult relationship, it is not the immediate physical attraction, but rather the emotional compatibility that brings a couple closer.

Beware of love at first sight. You may feel that your case is very different, and that you have found the person you were looking for to make a life companion. You may be right, but experience has shown there are greater chances that you are wrong. Feelings change with time. The excitement fades away as one weighs the pros and cons of the relationship with an unbiased mind, and the true perspective becomes clear. No relationship should be hurried with.

Understanding Love

All of us need to be loved. We cannot really tell what it means to us, but we can immediately feel the lack of it. To be lovable, people go to great lengths to make themselves attractive to others through their clothes and personal charm, by being useful in their vocations, and through their money and material possessions. Each person has his own way of attracting love.

Love cannot be demanded; nor can one expect it through physical appearance alone. It cannot be effective if it is just a superficial interpersonal relationship. To be sincere, it must come from within. True love cannot be hidden, or disguised. It knows no reasoning, and overlooks the differences of colour, cast or creed. It is both intoxicating and overpowering. It gives strength to both the lover and the loved. The foundations of personal happiness are built on it.

Going Steady

Going steady with the same person has its setbacks. It immediately restricts contact with just one person, cutting short the valuable experience one gains by meeting and knowing many different people. Such relationships may also tend to bring a couple together more out of loneliness and sympathy for each other, rather than because they are emotionally compatible. With each one trying to compromise with personal feelings to avoid the heartbreak of the partner, it may eventually lead to an unhappy marriage. A closer relationship in a young couple may also lead them to intimate physical contact resulting in tension, or in a sexual union, and may be even a premature marriage against will.

Even if the couple is mature enough to understand the various issues involved, and may be willing to break the relationship in good time, a certain amount of heartbreak is imminent when such ties are severed.

With no two individuals alike, no hard or fast rules can be fixed for human relationships. Meeting more people awakens one's awareness of different views, and helps one mature emotionally. Only with experience as one gains more self-confidence, and begins to understand the problems involved in adult man-woman relationships, would it be all right to get involved with a single person with the ultimate aim of getting married.

Kissing, Necking and Petting

What part does kissing, necking and petting play when young adults fall in love? Are these necessary? If so, then to what extent should one indulge in them? These problems perplex most young people.

With young couples beginning to understand and like each other, it is natural for them to desire some physical contact. It may begin with sitting close to each other in a restaurant or cinema hall, holding hands, or even walking in the park with arms around each other. This physical contact is quite different from the one each may have known as children loving their parents, brothers and sisters, or even meeting a friend with open arms. When a couple begin to like each other, even holding hands can be very pleasurable, sending sensations throughout the body. This often tempts the couple to experiment further with each other.

The first attempts at kissing and necking by a young couple may be no more than a small gesture of personal affection. Such show of affection can become stronger with more intense kissing, with tongues penetrating into each other's mouths, with kissing of the face, the ears, the neck, and even lower parts of the body. With the thrilling sensations one experiences this can set a chain reaction going with a growing desire for still closer contact, eventually ending up with an urgent desire for sexual intercourse. Such is the consequence of heavy kissing, necking and petting.

Young people should indulge in petting with great self-restraint. It should be a form of expression of personal affection and liking for each other, and should not be indulged in as a complete session, as many young couples tend to do. Excessive petting without fulfilment of sexual desire can be very frustrating, making one edgy and irritable. If a couple develops techniques to gratify each other without normal intercourse, over a period it may result in a habit that can affect normal married life. To keep petting within safe limits, avoid being alone for long periods. Go to places where you are not alone by yourselves, or go on joint dates, making a foursome. The couple must understand personal limitations, and must never go near the point of no return. While young men should particularly realise their responsibility, young women can play a significant role as they are slow to arouse, and yet prone to suffer if they make mistakes.

Physical attraction does help to hold two people together, and must occupy a reasonable place in life. Holding hands, being close to each other, or even an occasional kiss may be all right, but the real purpose of togetherness is to grow emotionally, and to learn to understand the mature adult relationship which leads one to marriage. Self-restraint is an essential feature of civilised society.

Sexual Love

Sexual love in unmarried couples is no more than a search for temporary thrills experienced in a spirit of experimentation. Young men advocate it because they have the urgent need to find an outlet for their aggressive sexual desire, and have apparently nothing to lose. These men assert that everyone is doing it, and why shouldn't they? Some girls are gullible, and give in because they do not wish to be the odd person out. Others may give in willingly because they have a foolish notion that it will help them in becoming more popular amongst friends. Some give in to experiment with the unknown. For most, it may happen rather too suddenly after a session of heavy petting. The need for expression of sexual desire may have gained momentum gradually, and once having taken a firm grip, there may have been no going back. Many of these affairs are sudden, secret, and on stolen time, without any aim or purpose. The couple realise it too late that they have been carried away by their feelings, and that also related to this issue are problems of pregnancy, contraception and venereal disease.

One needs to be patient and understanding to make sexual adjustments in married life. These can be made only when there is complete emotional involvement between the couple. The pleasure a married couple derives from a sexual union is not only from the physical union, but also from the deep-seated emotional ties that develop from sharing of many common everyday problems and interests.

Everyone grows up with certain personal values, and stands to gain or lose by them. Emotional maturity demands that every young adult place certain restraints upon personal feelings. The restraint differentiates love from passion. Like other adult values, double standards begin to take root when those very young men who advocate pre-marital sexual experience look for virgin brides. Since it is the young girl who stands to lose the most, it is for her to set limits, and make it clear that she goes by certain values, and also expects them to be respected. Any sensible person will understand and appreciate her viewpoint, and not make an effort to go any further than is acceptable to her.

Mature Love

How can one be sure that the feelings that bring a couple close are those of mature love, and not of temporary physical attraction, or infatuation? The answer to this question would put the minds of many lovers at peace. A mature relationship between a couple leads them to settle down to build a home and rear a family. An important consideration before the couple should be whether a permanent relationship would help *them* find fulfilment of their personal hopes and aspirations. Mature love does not envisage personal fulfilment only. It emphasises mutual fulfilment, and growth of both partners.

Another consideration should be whether a person is in love with the partner, or with the circumstances which surround him or her. The days of courting can be very deceptive because they put forth a person who is out to attract with personal charm and friendliness, but without any responsibilities to share. Real life is very different. There will be many problems to be resolved, and many fears and obstacles to be overcome. Since an individual's response to the same problem can be very different, one needs to consider how the two feel about them together. Can you sort them out together? Many young people deceive themselves that with love they can smooth out many an awkward problem. This is not true. We need to look at human relationships for what they are, and not as what we would like them to be.

Finally, we need to remember that mature love encourages intelligent self-expression in the partner, and creates an atmosphere in which the couple can find more happiness together than each can find separately. This form of love grows gradually with the sharing of similar hopes and aspirations, with a determination to face individual fears and problems together, and out of mutual trust, respect and consideration for each other.

Points to ponder...

- ❑ Love is the greatest, yet the most misunderstood, emotion.
- ❑ We need love throughout life.
- ❑ Differentiate between love and infatuation.
- ❑ True love gives strength to both the lover and the loved.
- ❑ Dating aims at developing companionship amongst young couples.
- ❑ Mature love aims at a couple finding more happiness together than what each can find individually.

❖❖

12

Self-employment

"If you would have a faithful servant, and one that you like, serve yourself."

—Franklin

Many young people do succeed in finding reasonable jobs. Many do not. Many do find jobs, but unfortunately, do not find them satisfying. The remuneration may be low. A more common reason may be that the job may not offer the challenges and prospects that young people look forward to, particularly after specialised training. Besides, with good jobs not easy to come by, no young person can wait indefinitely for one, and may therefore have to turn to self-employment.

Almost in every sphere of activity, there are thousands of young people who are trained to undertake specialised jobs, but surprisingly, they are afraid to become self-employed. The fault does not lie entirely with their specialised training. It may be due to lack of confidence in putting their knowledge to use by themselves. Many factors influence successful self-employment. If youngsters could understand them, many of their secret fears would vanish. They could be usefully self-employed. Let us discuss some of the important aspects of the problem in this chapter.

Opportunities for Self-employment

The opportunities for self-employment are almost unlimited. This sounds rather incredible, but it is true. Almost in every sphere of life, a person who has received a fair amount of education can do well, provided of course that he can fulfil other basic needs. An opportunity is no more than an inspiring thought which comes into the mind, and tells us of a useful product or service we can provide to the public in return for a reasonable remuneration. Human needs are unlimited, and if we can learn to understand and fulfil these needs, opportunities will continue to grow forever.

If you are in search of opportunities for self-employment, study human needs. Ask yourself: What new products can make life more comfortable and efficient in the community? Can you manufacture or supply any of these products? Can you improve upon any of the existing products? If you cannot, perhaps there might be some new service you may be able to provide. In answering these questions, you will need to exercise your imagination. The more you meet people and understand their problems, the better you will realise how you can provide a product, or service, to fulfil these needs. You should not be afraid to copy an idea from a product or service marketed elsewhere. If it has succeeded in another community, there are fair chances of success in your community, provided of course that the needs of the people are similar.

One should also understand that many needs are not needs in the literal sense of the word. They may be simple desires or fancies. Many people with some imagination have learnt to play upon these, and gone ahead to provide products and services to fulfil them. The opportunities for self-employment in this direction are many. Innumerable novelties, fashions, designs, etc., are the results of such enterprise. They result in a turnover of millions of rupees a year. Our imagination can give us unlimited ideas, and upon these depend the continued growth of a community and society in general, raising the standard of living of the common man. It is always the most imaginative and enterprising young person who learns to score quickly and surely.

Selecting the Correct Line

Once a person can learn to recognise opportunities for self-employment, literally dozens of good ideas that can be adapted into full-time occupations come to mind. The ideas can be classified into two categories. The first one aims at selling products or services, and the second one at manufacturing products of interest to people. Since needs vary from place to place, one will have to adjust the ideas to suit personal needs.

Local requirements offer the most feasible ideas for self-employment. Depending upon personal aptitude, one could start a local newspaper or a weekly news magazine, establish a modern laundering or dry cleaning unit, start a home delivery service, or perhaps just open a small retail store. If one is so qualified, there is scope for establishing advisory and consultative services as a lawyer, an accountant, or a marketing consultant. If there are local novelties or specialties, they offer sales potential in other towns, and sometimes even in other countries. Mail order sales can open the entire world as a suitable market if the product is of universal interest. Distribution of products of reliable companies in one's own community offers great possibilities as, many times, exclusive sales rights for special products can be obtained on territory basis, ensuring one of a steady business.

Manufacturing offers both challenges and problems. The need for import substitution has opened many new fields of manufacturing industries, but many of these require specialised knowledge. Some people manufacture an entire product. However, there are many that take advantage of existing manufacturing facilities, and get many of the components manufactured elsewhere, and assemble the product to sell it under a special trade name. Many states organise special facilities in guidance and training for the opening of small-scale industries. Many readymade schemes are also available for prospective entrepreneurs. One can study them and, with some modifications, adapt them to suit personal needs. For ladies interested in self-employment, manufacture of readymade clothes, handwork and novelty items, hosiery, knitted garments, embroidered articles, etc. offer great potential for self-employment.

Catering to the needs of people living in rural areas offers great possibilities for useful work. There is need for a vast number of products and services, useful in fields and homes. Many people would like to use special equipment on rental basis. The need for new and useful products is always there. Re-packing of seeds and chemicals in convenient packs is a boon for small farmers. There are millions of rural homes that could use many useful products that are so far available only in towns and cities.

One could go on indefinitely with innumerable ideas for self-employment. They have stood the test of time, and could succeed at other places. However, one needs to draw a line when an individual has found an opening of his choice. Personal aptitudes and capabilities vary from one individual to another. With that, the choice of a suitable vocation will also vary. Consider as many lines as you would like to, but with each consideration, go on narrowing the choice until you come to that single line on which you can finally set your heart.

Personal Evaluation for Success

Before you decide to become your own employer, make certain that you have the basic qualifications to make a success of it. You will need to be frank and honest with yourself. For your own sake, try to evaluate the situation correctly. You will be both the employer and the employee. Eventually the responsibility of all rights and wrongs will rest upon you. It is surely going to be an uphill task in the beginning.

Ask yourself if you have the initiative and drive to try out the new idea. Will you enjoy carrying it through? Do you consider yourself a production man, or a salesman? Are you technically qualified to undertake the work? Are you going to rely upon outside technical help? Will you be willing to put in hard work, very often sacrificing personal leisure, and even working late hours? Are you enthusiastic enough to keep going even when others would be too discouraged to continue? Can you get along well with people? The answers to these questions will give you a good idea of your chances of success at becoming your own boss.

Write down the answers on paper, think of them again at your leisure. Discuss the issue with your parents or with a close friend or relative whom you know to be reliable in his opinion about your capabilities. Their opinion can be very useful. You will need to be realistic about it yourself because nobody knows you better than you. When you take a realistic and practical view about it, even if you are lacking in some ways, you can ensure success by making up for shortcomings.

Evaluating the Product or Service

Once you have made up your mind as to what you would like to do, it is time to investigate the potentialities of the product or service you have to offer. To play safe, do not rely upon your personal convictions only. Base your decisions on facts. You would need to be ruthlessly unbiased and honest about your observations and findings. Only then can others be attracted to pay for what you have to offer.

At the very outset, you should remember that your rewards depend upon the sale of your product or service to others. Therefore, it is essential that the offer must be for something attractive and useful. It must be reasonably priced. After making an assessment of the need your product or service will fulfil, ask your parents and friends about it. Your aim should not be to convince others of your assessment, but to study their viewpoint.

The people you need to contact next are those through whom you hope to market your products or service, or those who will be interested in them as actual users. If it is a product that is being introduced for the first time, take a sample to the wholesalers, the retailers and the consumers independently, and ask their opinion about it. Ask them about its utility, and a possible demand. Finally, you could ask them what price would they pay for it. If it is a product that is already selling in the market, ask them to make comparisons. Enquire as to what is the normal trade discount expected by the wholesaler and the retailers.

It would also be useful if you could discuss your product or service with people like bank managers, advertising executives, and a professional accountant. These people have great insight into various types of trades, and can provide you with a lot of useful information. Marketing consultants feel that if the response to your enquiries is eighty per cent in your favour, the project is worthwhile and you can go ahead.

Preparing the Plan

With a go-ahead signal from all sides, your next job is to prepare a plan as to how you go about your new project. If you are offering personal services, or starting a selling concern, you know what margin of profit to expect. In this case, you will need to plan how you can attract the maximum clientele. There are certain ethics of every profession, and you will need to observe them. Normally success comes gradually with increasing experience.

If you are introducing a new product, you will need to consider whether you would like to manufacture it yourself or like to get it manufactured by somebody else, and sell it yourself under a special trade name. You will also have to consider whether you are going to sell it only in your own town or other towns. If so, how are you going to market it? You could sell it through established wholesalers and retailers, but in that case, you must study trade journals and advertisements in the national newspapers, and get in touch with them well in advance. Selling is the basis of all enterprise, and you must give it ample thought before proceeding with anything else.

The cost of the product or service that you offer is most important. It must take into consideration the manufacturing costs, the selling costs, and a fair profit. In the beginning, your margin may not be substantial, but with gradual development you must get a fair return for your labour and capital. Above all else, your cost structure must be similar to those who market similar products and services.

Since most newcomers to business and trade have no idea of the complete regulation of costs, it is necessary that the plans you make must be conservative in investing in the new line. You will do well to print good business stationery, letterheads, advertising literature, etc., because these are your personal messengers to prospective customers, but do not hire any unnecessary office or factory site, or staff. Keep expenses at the barest minimum until the business can pay for the little extras. Emphasise upon the quality of the product or service, and not upon style. The ultimate success is not reflected by the style you maintain but by the profits you earn.

Financing the Plan

Many good plans are abandoned for the simple reason that there may be no money to execute them. This should not be the case. One does need to muster personal resources to make a beginning, but once established, it should not be difficult to raise loans to bring about useful expansion. However, a loan should never be raised unless one is certain that it can be repaid within a certain specified period. With a good personal standing it should not be difficult to raise a reasonable loan from friends and relatives. If one is technically qualified, and has a good plan, banks readily help with loan facilities at reasonable rates of interest.

If the project is rather huge, and though promising, cannot be executed without substantial finances, the only solution is in taking up a financing partner. Many people are willing to finance good projects, but often have their own conditions to impose. It may not be possible to find such a partner easily, and advertising in papers offers the best solution in that case.

The Need to Go Slow

Many business concerns close down in the very first year of their existence. Unimaginative planning is a common problem. However, the extravagance of spending on unprofitable items has let down many a newcomer. One just cannot overemphasise the need to go very slow in the beginning. Try to operate from your own home, if possible. Do as much as you can personally. In any new venture, it is essential that the risk involved be kept at the barest minimum. When the business begins to pay, you can expand because then you can be confident that the venture will pay for itself.

Some Common Problems

Self-employment is not without its share of problems. Every young person embarking upon a personal business venture will do well to understand and anticipate them to ensure a smooth beginning, and trouble-free progress.

For many trades there are certain restrictions imposed by the Municipal Boards, the State Governments, and even the Central Government. These restrictions should not immediately frighten a young person starting a new business because many of these are imposed in the interests of health and sanitation or to facilitate the collection of taxes. It would therefore be necessary to enquire, and suitable permission sought, before making a beginning. The best people to contact about these restrictions are those who are already engaged in similar lines. Trade associations can offer very valuable advice in this direction. For taxation purposes, one can seek the advice of consultants who specialise in this.

In any new trade there are bound to be moments of discouragement, frustration and heartbreak. One needs to guard against these weaker moments as many people give up their struggle to succeed at this stage. It is undoubtedly a lonely uphill journey. One must remember that only those who persevere reach the top. It will entail hard work, but it will be paid for through better rewards.

Another vital problem that young entrepreneurs need to be aware of is that trends in business keep changing. The product or service you may offer today may be outdated in five years. Alternatively, the competition may become so great that it may not remain worthwhile to continue, as the returns may not be reasonable. To keep ahead of competition and the times, one needs to be observant. Keep up with the trends. Regularly go through trade journals. Plan ahead of time. Keep your plan flexible. Give the people what they want, and not what you think they should have.

Expanding the Work

With success achieved on a small scale, you will surely want to expand your business. Do it gradually. There should be phased expansion so that neither do the investments mount up suddenly, nor the sales lag behind. Since the demand for your products or services will rise only gradually, your expansion programme can envisage a proportionate growth. To meet the growing financial requirements you could plough back a certain percentage of the profits each year. With good results to add to your confidence, you could also avail of various credit facilities available to enterprising young entrepreneurs.

To boost sales in an expanding business you will need to advertise more freely. A little extra cost in getting the services of a professional advertising agency is worthwhile. If you decide to write your own advertising copy, make it short, to the point, and be honest with your claims. It must be attractive, but certainly not deceptive. Advertise in newspapers and magazines read mostly by those whom your products or services will interest.

A point of utmost importance is that you should not expand your business at the cost of quality of the products or services you offer. Instead of bringing down quality, you could charge a slightly higher price, if it is justifiable. Work constantly to improve your products or services. This really means that you need to improve your own performance. Do not forget that those who give a little more value in the form of quality and service for the same money continue to attract more clientele. All big business houses grew this way. So can you.

Points to ponder...

- ❑ One cannot keep waiting for a job.
- ❑ Self-employment holds the key to a satisfying career.
- ❑ Understand human needs. Fulfil them to build a career.
- ❑ Assess your strengths and weaknesses.
- ❑ Prepare a realistic plan. Act with courage.
- ❑ Grow slowly.

❖❖

13

Preparing for Marriage

"The happiness of married life depends upon making small sacrifices with readiness and cheerfulness."

—Selden

With young people coming of age it is natural for them to marry, and settle down to raise a family. Through marriage, each partner looks forward to find that happiness which one cannot find independently. Through trial and error, many succeed in finding the emotional fulfilment they are in search of through this delicate relationship. Unfortunately, many couples fail to find happiness in marriage.

Marriage apparently offers many promises of mutual fulfilment to each partner. However, when it comes to living from day to day, it is not without its many complexities.

Those who enjoy a successful marriage confirm that nothing could be more blissful than being happily married. Happiness in marriage stimulates creativity, and raises each partner to great heights of achievement. However, the need for two individuals to live together and share everything creates problems that are not always easy to anticipate. No two individuals are alike, and there are bound to be differences of opinion on many issues. Many factors affect this delicate relationship. People who are willing to understand these, and adapt themselves to the varying circumstances, should not find it difficult to avoid the many pitfalls which lead one to failure.

Understanding Marriage

Marriage is no bed of roses. It immediately places many responsibilities on both the husband and the wife. In exchange for its promise of emotional fulfilment and bliss, it demands many sacrifices. To a certain degree, personal independence is lost. One needs to give selflessly before expecting to find happiness later.

Marriage assigns added roles to every individual. Instead of the role of an independent person, one begins to play the more difficult role of a husband or a wife, each of which requires complex responsibilities towards the other. Later, when the children arrive, there is the difficult role of parenthood. After marriage, even the role as a citizen carries greater significance as society begins to expect a greater show of responsibility in day-to-day life. On many occasions, partners may have to change roles, or even share the varied responsibilities involved. It is creating a fair balance of these responsibilities between each partner that ensures happiness in marriage.

Marriage aims at providing mutual companionship and emotional security to the couple. However, just as human beings cannot be perfect, we cannot expect complete perfection in this relationship either. Marriage has many in-built problems, and one needs to learn to anticipate and cope with them. Since many factors are involved in this two-way relationship, let us consider them one by one.

Expectations in Marriage

Many marriages run into trouble because one of the partners, or sometimes even both, expect too much out of it. Unfortunately, for many young people marriage means an easy way to achieve many of their personal desires. These people entertain great expectations of their partners, but human nature being what it is, it is not long before they find themselves disillusioned and frustrated.

To play safe, keep your expectations within reasonable limits. Do not expect your partner to be a superhuman being. Every person entertains certain hopes and aspirations. To your partner these are as important as yours are to you. If you want your dreams to turn into reality, you will need to fulfil the desires of your partner to avoid a clash of individual interests. Very often young people feel that love is the central element of a successful marriage. If that exists, there is little else to worry about. It is true that love is the greatest of all emotions. It can help in sorting out the most difficult problems. However, how many people can really recognise true love? Love cannot exist without many other seemingly insignificant requisites that make the relationship mutually satisfying. Thoughtfulness of the needs of the partner promotes emotional security in marriage, but such bonds grow gradually as the couple learn to share their lives like mature adults.

Selecting the Right Partner

Does selecting the right partner ensure a happy married life? Perhaps, yes. However, the issue is not as simple as it appears to be. While on one hand one may be emotionally involved with the partner, on the other, one cannot ignore practical considerations. Again, since it is not easy to judge people accurately in a short period, it is difficult to predict how a person will respond in an intimate relationship like marriage.

Even in the present age, not all young people may be free of parental bonds to select a partner independently. There is a certain amount of parental dependence. One's personal circumstances may not make it possible. Whatever be the case, experience has shown that both arranged and love marriages have a fair chance of success, provided the couple understand the responsibilities of married life. In most cases, parents and well-wishers are helpful in suggesting suitable matches. However, some may still prefer to select one from amongst the many people one may come across through one's vocation, or in social life.

Before one can consider the several aspects of selecting a partner, there is need for evaluation of personal hopes and aspirations. Everyone has certain needs and expectations of marriage. Whatever they may be, one needs to define them clearly. And later, as one comes across prospective matches, one can compare as to what degree one can hope to fulfil these needs, and also to what extent one needs to compromise with circumstances.

In selecting a partner, physical attraction draws immediate attention. However, there are many other considerations like family background, education, and individual concept of money. This is important because general living standards, food habits, and the approach towards earning and spending money can create many conflicts. One would also do well to enquire if the partner has any special expectations from marriage. It is perfectly normal to have them, but if the expectations of the couple clash in principle, it may not be without a detrimental effect on married life.

Willingness to adapt oneself to various circumstances is a great virtue, but we often tend to over-rate this quality both in ourselves, and in others. Emotions colour one's judgement, and very often it is assumed that certain shortcomings will easily be surmounted with love, but when it comes to everyday life, the situation may be just the reverse. It is therefore advisable that due consideration be given to obvious shortcomings in a proposal.

Many young people are afraid that they may make a wrong choice, and to play safe may decide to tread only on known territory, and opt to marry a cousin. Some communities accept such a choice, but most do not. And, rightly so too. Marriage between first and second cousins may ensure better understanding between the couple, and better prospects of happiness in marriage, but such a relationship is harmful for children born of such wedlock. According to the laws of inheritance, when close relatives marry, recessive genes (controlling undesired characteristics) come to the surface, sometimes causing serious abnormalities in the children.

On another extreme are those young people who may decide to marry someone outside their own caste or community. Such marriages are on the increase. They have a fair chance of success, provided some of the obvious shortcomings have been given due consideration. In such marriages, both partners need to be more understanding because of the different family backgrounds and living patterns they may be used to. Since such marriages are often the result of mutual friendship and courting, they are often between young people who not only share common views on many subjects, but are also broadminded and tolerant of each other's personal background. However, such marriages have lesser chance of success in the atmosphere of a joint family. Personal religious faiths and customs may also sometimes clash in such marriages. This is of particular significance as it may cause unforeseen misunderstandings about the bringing up of children, specially when each partner may have leanings towards different religious faiths and beliefs. Although of lesser importance, some couples have experienced difficulties relating to differences in language and food habits. As is obvious, inter-communal marriages require a series of compromises on various issues. Only when one partner is willing to give in a little more than the other, can smooth sailing be ensured.

Getting Engaged

An engagement is an official announcement amongst friends and relatives that a young couple has agreed to marry in the near future. The announcement may be made at an elaborate ceremony attended by hundreds of people, or may be a quiet affair with the young man slipping a ring on the finger of his prospective bride. In some cases, the wedding soon follows the engagement. In others, it may extend over a longer period. On an average, this period may be six to twelve months.

This period offers the couple the right opportunity to meet and understand each other better. Even the more conservative parents shed a part of their hesitation in allowing the couple to meet on their own. Many of the problems can be sorted out at this stage. This is the time to gauge each other's expectations from marriage, and if it would be possible to find fulfilment through the relationship. From the general attitude towards various subjects, one can tell whether the approach of a partner is selfish, or otherwise. However, both the partners must make a fair allowance for one setback. The meetings of the couple may be formal and, therefore, the appearances that each partner puts up will be the very best of him, or her. This can be very deceptive. Marriage brings the couple intimately close, and each partner should therefore look at the other as he or she is in real life, and not in those fleeting moments that the couple are together.

With the young couple physically attracted to each other, and with many of the usual barriers between them going down through better understanding of each other, they may be tempted to experiment with more ardent kissing, necking and petting. "What is wrong with it? Are we not getting married soon?" Most young men seem to place a stress upon this outlook. However, young people who value the sanctity of marriage know that emotional fulfilment is more important than a physical outlet, and understand that it is best to wait until they get married.

Would it be all right to break an engagement if one of the partners feels that he, or she, may not find mutual fulfilment in the relationship? Yes, it would certainly be preferable to a lifelong unhappy union. This may have its own repercussions. A broken engagement may mean a broken heart for the other person. In such a case, the situation must be handled very tactfully. Both partners must understand the areas of differences. They must appreciate how the differences are likely to create problems in married life. When the disparities are clear, the two families or some mutual friends can always be helpful in settling the matter amicably for the young couple.

Preparing for Marriage

Besides the exchange of past experiences, one subject that dominates the conversation of any courting couple engaged to marry soon is the home they will together make after getting married. Unfortunately, since both partners are eager to impress each other, they tend to be showy and ostentatious, leading to unnecessary extravagance. The parents of the bride and the groom do like to give presents to help the couple to set up a home of their own. However, very often many such articles are purchased for which neither of the partners has any use. A lot of money that could have been better utilised in some other form by the couple is lost this way.

The eagerness of the parents to buy the bride whatever she desires gives many a young girl the impression that, for her, marriage is the beginning of an era of plenty. She begins to feel that she will be able to get all that she desires. For some time even the groom lives in a false world when he gets presents of expensive clothes and accessories which he cannot normally afford in everyday life from his own earnings. Suddenly, one day the couple wakes up to the harsh reality that they must live within their means.

In preparing for marriage, young people should not overlook the pattern of life that awaits them after marriage. Only such clothes and necessities must be purchased that can be put to the best use. It is true that parents may not always be willing to purchase such gifts. However, their generosity should not be misused. If they are financially in a position to give more, but you are not sure as to what you would like to buy, ask them to keep the money reserved until you have the right use for it. Later, on many occasions, the couple will need it for necessities they may not be aware of before marriage.

To avoid unnecessary duplication of presents from friends also, many couples are frank in discussing the issue with friends earlier, or even accepting cash gifts. If the couple take a frank and straightforward attitude towards preparing for marriage, the same money and efforts can give both partners greater happiness from what they buy for their home.

The Marriage Ceremony

The law does not recognise a man and woman as husband and wife even if they are living together. To be accepted as husband and wife they must be married in keeping with certain customs and traditions clearly recognised by the law of the land.

The marriage ceremony may be as simple a ceremony as a couple signing the register before the local Registrar of Marriages, or may extend the day long with multifarious ceremonies in keeping with individual religious beliefs. Customs vary with religions, and from place to place, and from one community to another. With them, the mechanics of the marriage ceremony too may differ. The choice as to what is best is that of the couple and the parents. Although such occasions are normally accompanied with great pomp and splendour, and with feasting and celebrations, experience has shown that the simpler the ceremony, the more enjoyable it is for everyone.

The Honeymoon

There is difference of opinion as to whether a couple should go for a honeymoon after marriage. Those who advocate it, contend that it gives the couple an opportunity to be away from the interruptions and responsibilities of a home. It gives them time to understand and know each other better to enable easier adjustments in married life. A honeymoon also provides the right atmosphere for consummation of marriage, and for intimacy to grow between the couple.

On the other hand, others feel that when the couple is already courting, they have had enough opportunity to understand each other. Besides, one cannot hope to learn to make adjustments only during the honeymoon. After all, life is an everyday affair, and adjustments must be made as one continues to learn about each other throughout life. Therefore, the expenditure on a honeymoon may not be a wise investment.

The ultimate choice rests with the couple concerned. Opinions will always vary. One must decide what would be most suitable. It is true that money spent on a honeymoon could be used to buy some useful items at home. However, we cannot overlook the fact that it offers a happy holiday for the couple. On return, they can begin their new life with additional zest and fervour.

Consummation of Marriage

Amidst the great pleasure and happiness that a couple experience on getting married, there is one anxiety which gnaws at the mind of every young person – the fear of what the first sexual experience with the partner is going to be like. Some look forward to the pleasures it promises to offer, but most young people entertain secret fears about their personal performance. It must be admitted that this anxiety is not altogether ill founded. This first experience has deep implications in paving a path for making adjustments for a satisfying physical relationship between the husband and wife for the rest of their life.

Nature has placed certain limitations in making this first experience a perfect sexual union for the couple. In fact, sometimes it may even be a rather disturbing experience. The fear of pregnancy is another cause of anxiety in the couple. Whatever the cause may be, the couple will do well to understand that a certain amount of anxiety is normal when two people are entering into a new and intimate relationship. Each must help the other in getting rid of hidden fears. The correct attitude takes away the unpleasantness out of the experience, and may make it rather satisfying for the couple.

How soon after marriage should the couple have their first sexual union? Many couples are at a loss to answer this. Some believe that marriage must be consummated the very first night the couple is together. Others think it might be better to wait a little. Experience has shown that it is best to wait until both the partners are mentally prepared for the experience. Couples who may have been courting for sometime, and know each other fairly well, may be quite prepared for it on the first night of their marriage, but others may need to wait. Whichever way it is, patience, particularly on the part of the husband, pays rich dividends in establishing a firm foundation for a satisfying physical relationship throughout life.

The husband needs to understand that as compared to him, the wife may not only be shy to undress before him, but that by nature women are passive, and slow to arouse and desire a sexual union. When she gives herself up to him, she is voluntarily giving him all that she can. To win her psychologically the husband must convince the wife of his love, fidelity and willingness to keep her happy. With the mental barriers fading away, physical contact becomes easier. Kissing, necking and fondling further pave the way to make her desire a union with the husband.

Despite complete understanding and cooperation between the couple, the first sexual union may still be far from satisfying for the couple. Even if all goes well, the wife may still not find the experience enjoyable for the first few times. Whatever be the case, it calls for patience and understanding on the part of both partners. They must realise that problems are normal. Only with experience will both learn to make the sexual union mutually satisfying and pleasurable.

Developing Mutual Understanding

No couple is completely compatible at the time of marriage. Differences will always be there. What makes these differences less significant in some marriages as compared to others is the willingness of the couple to develop areas of mutual understanding in their married life. Many obvious questions arise in early married life. Who should be the boss? The husband, or the wife? Should there be equality? If so, then in what areas of life can equality work?

While tradition has given man the privilege of being the head of the family, the latest concept is that of equality where both the husband and the wife share the responsibility of the family. While the man is accepted as the head of the family, the wife takes the pride of place as the head of the household.

It is necessary that there should be one boss so that firm decisions can be taken. The new freedom gives the woman the right to express her individuality. A woman may accept being dominated by her husband, but certainly not crushed by him. She has her needs of appreciation for what she contributes towards the welfare of the family. Once a couple can understand each other's needs, and develop interests that do not clash, mutual understanding will grow, making the bonds of marriage stronger.

Communication in Marriage

The efficiency of any relationship is directly related to the quality of communication between the persons concerned. A married couple communicates in many ways. Much can be communicated not only through spoken words, but also through a glance, a clasp of the hand, or just the nod of the head, or movement of the eyes. Still a failure in communicating efficiently has turned many a marriage into an unhappy affair.

Young married people need to understand that despite the best efforts some problems cannot be easily resolved. Communicating efficiently is one of them. Words can mean different things to various people. Besides, the tone and the pitch of the voice can alter the meaning of a sentence. Again, most people are not good listeners, and will be absentminded even when you think they are not. Emotions can also cloud one's expression and understanding. Those who are not comfortable with words may revolt with an uneasy silence that can punish the other as severely as caustic words.

The secret of good communication in marriage lies in not allowing misunderstandings to accumulate. Settle them as often as necessary. Do it at an appropriate time. There always are moments when people are more receptive than at other times. If you are at fault, do not let swallowing your pride hurt you. It will be in your own interest. If you are not satisfied with a compromise, explain why. Do not pretend to be a martyr. Talk reasonably. Be a willing listener. You must constantly strive to keep misunderstandings out of your married life.

Sex in Marriage

Sex plays a significant role in keeping a marriage alive. Good sexual adjustment is an integral part of a happy marriage. Whether the sexual relations are mutually satisfying will depend upon the personal attitude of the couple. Unfortunately, many young couples develop attitudes that may not be conducive to making reasonable adjustments thereby wrecking the chances of success of an otherwise happy marriage.

All young people need to understand that sex is both creative and recreative. It is a form of expression of love and affection for each other. The pleasure that ensues from it helps in combating the tensions of everyday living, and in strengthening the emotional bonds that tie a couple together.

Sexual relations do not become mutually satisfying immediately after marriage. It may take months, or even years, for the couple to understand each other's body language, and to enjoy the art of sexual love. Many never learn it at all. Many people turn to books about sex in the hope of acquiring the requisite knowledge. Many of these books are good, and impart useful knowledge. One needs to remember that what is written in these books is generalised, and must be accepted only after due consideration. Sexual relations between the couple are a very personal affair. What some people like may not please others. It is, therefore, important to understand that mutual adjustments can be made only by developing greater understanding of each other's liking and preferences, by promoting a feeling of security, and through greater emotional attachment. Sexual needs vary at different stages of life, but when there is a continued willingness to make adjustments, mutual satisfaction is achieved.

Sex Outside Marriage

If sex in marriage can be completely satisfying to the couple, then why is it that sometimes a partner, or even both, turns to sex outside marriage? This can happen under varying circumstances. If it happens on a stray occasion, it may be due to no more than a temporary loss of balance of the mind of the person concerned. The reason may be more deep-seated if it is repeated often. This does not indicate that the couple have failed to give due importance to mutual sexual fulfilment, or have not been able to provide emotional security to each other. Sometimes a partner may go astray to use sex as a weapon against the other.

If one fails to find pleasure from sex in marriage, then sex outside marriage is hardly a worthwhile solution. Society does not accept it. Even if it did, extramarital sex cannot provide the sublime pleasure which sex with a married partner can. The pleasure does not come from the physical contact only, but from the emotional bonds that bind the couple as they share each other's life.

Husband-Wife Quarrels

No marriage is free from occasional quarrels between the husband and wife. However, these quarrels may assume an unhappy form endangering not only the marriage, but also the happiness of the couple and their children. This sets one wondering if these quarrels can altogether be avoided. If so, how can this be achieved? If we cannot avoid them altogether, then can we at least ensure that they do not assume an unhappy magnitude in one's life?

Considering the problem in a wide sense, experience has shown that these quarrels serve a useful purpose in providing an outlet for the tension that builds up in a close relationship like marriage. If this tension were not to find an easy outlet, it can affect the physical and emotional health of the couple. The quarrels also serve to keep the partners alert to each other's needs, and very often stimulate one to do better the next time. In reality the problem is not that husband-wife quarrels are bad, but that most couples do not have the correct attitude towards this aspect of married life.

When the interests of two individuals clash, it is natural for them to quarrel. If one of the partners, or even both, suppress their feelings to avoid the unpleasantness of a mild tiff now and then, the chances are that they are only temporarily putting up a false appearance. Eventually, the suppressed feelings emerge as ill health, or as an unbecoming volcanic outburst far worse than all the little quarrels put together. Never suppress your feelings. If you are indignant about something, do not hesitate to express it to your partner. Do try to understand the other person's point of view also. Discuss the issue point by point. Do not mix up the issues, or try to make your arguments stronger by raising your voice. Be calm and tactful. You will find it easy to compromise intelligently in married life. You can learn to sort out your problems without hitting the partner below the belt by arguing unreasonably. Occasional petty quarrels help cement the emotional bonds between you and your partner, ensuring greater happiness in marriage.

Children

After marriage there is the addition of a baby into the family. This will entail many adjustments. The baby will need to be fed, clothed, kept clean, and above all, kept happy and secure. This has financial implications. It also means that the attention of the wife will be divided between the child and the husband. Some men mistake this division of attention as a deliberate effort of the wife to avoid them, thus causing unnecessary jealousy and misunderstandings. A baby means a more restricted social life for the couple. With the children growing up, the problems do not get completely resolved, but just change their shape. New problems take the place of old ones. Adjustments need to be made from time to time. If the marriage is to be kept alive, it is necessary that the couple understand their responsibilities, and keep each other emotionally satisfied and happy.

Attitude Towards Money

Money is important to both the husband and the wife. When views about earning and spending begin to clash, it has a detrimental effect upon the marriage. In the present times, many wives are as much earners as their husbands. There has to be a reasonable understanding regarding use of their earnings. Even when the wife does not personally earn in return for her contribution towards managing the household, she may insist on having a say about how the family earnings should be utilised.

Concepts of how money should be used vary from one person to another. Since childhood experiences about money affect adult attitudes about it, many of the concepts are deep-rooted, and compromising with them is not easy. One's peace of mind is affected directly by one's financial position. It is, therefore, imperative that the couple develop mutual understanding about their finances early in marriage so that it may not act as an obstacle in their happiness.

Making Marriage a Success

No rigid rules can be prescribed for making a marriage successful. Just as no two persons are alike, no two marriages are the same. Differences continue to provide the spice of life. Physical attraction alone is not enough to keep a marriage alive. Each partner must understand what marriage means to the other. The secret hopes and aspirations of each partner must find an intelligent outlet. When the couple is united in matrimony, it does not mean that each partner has shed individuality, or overcome personal needs. It only means that the differences of opinions do not arouse resentment in the other, but are respected. Each helps the other fulfil personal interests.

Marriage brings down many barriers that exist between a man and woman. However, there will always be the need to respect the individual yearning for occasional privacy. This must be honoured. As emotional bonds grow with time, this need gradually vanishes. Since living is a dynamic experience, one is always changing either for the better, or for the worse. To ensure success, learn to observe and adapt to personal convenience.

Use persuasion. Learn to accept your partner as he or she is. Never demand the partner change. People are averse to deliberate change. If you feel that a change is for the better, explain why, and lead the way by making it work in your own life. A mutual compromise makes marital ties stronger.

A successful marriage is not built upon a few great deeds or sacrifices. It depends upon many trifling things done for each other day after day without any obligation. Thoughtfulness strengthens marital bonds. Love always begets love.

Points to ponder...

- ❑ Keep your expectations from marriage within reasonable limits.
- ❑ Choosing the right partner in marriage involves many factors.
- ❑ Lasting relationships develop slowly through mutual understanding.
- ❑ Patience is the key to a happy physical relationship between a couple.
- ❑ Good communication and understanding keep a marriage alive.
- ❑ Do not suppress differences. Settle them in all fairness.
- ❑ A successful marriage is built upon small things done for each other day after day.

❖❖

14

Winning Popularity

"Fame is a vapour, popularity an accident; riches take wings... only one thing endures – character."

—Anon

Each one of us desires to be appreciated. We want to be popular among our friends and others. This is an inborn desire. Beginning from infancy, it never loses hold until the very end of life. It only changes form from one stage of life to another, and continues to guide our thoughts, feelings, actions and habits. The need for appreciation is important as it makes us feel wanted. It provides us with a feeling of security in an environment that is both selfish and competitive. Since it is a natural desire, we cannot completely overlook it. This desire can, like all other desires, motivate us to actions that are reasonable, or those that are not acceptable to society. There is, therefore, a need to understand various factors that influence this desire in our everyday life. This way we can channelise our thoughts and actions towards more progressive living.

Winning Immediate Attention

An infant gains immediate attention through crying. As he grows he begins to understand the need to give something in return for the expected attention and approval, and learns to smile and conform to the wishes of his parents and others. School brings him into contact with the wider world, and other forms of winning attention and appreciation begin to take shape in his daily life.

In adult life, the desire to wield power over others by gaining approval and appreciation begins to feature significantly in everyday life. Everyone pursues power to fulfil this desire in many ways. The most elementary form is through the show of physical strength. Since this has many obvious limitations in a civilised society, knowledge comes to the forefront as a greater source of power. From this emerges yet another form of power that one gains by occupying important positions in life. With rapid development all over the world, and with the growing materialistic values of life, money has become synonymous with power. As we all know, money is used in numerous ways to win immediate attention and approval of the people around us. Only a few have really understood the truth about gaining power by winning human goodwill.

Since young people learn to copy what they see, they adopt various methods of winning attention and power to suit individual needs and conditions. Some succeed in creating a pleasing effect. Many fail to do so. Little do these people understand that each form of power which is pursued in everyday life has its limitations.

Personal Image

The basic method all of us follow to win attention and popularity is to project an image that would gain the favourable approval of the maximum number of people we come across in everyday life. This is not easy. In real life, people do not project one image, but rather many images. The family, friends and people in general all think differently of the same person. What is still more significant is that what a person thinks of himself may be altogether different from what others think of him. The image one has of himself would be better than the impressions which others might have of him. To ensure a fair image, the aim should be to remove the parallax between the various images one casts in the minds of people. The methods young people employ to achieve this are similar to those used by elders in everyday life. It will be useful to note the methods young people adopt to fulfil their desire for appreciation.

Bragging

A method commonly used by young people from various spheres of life to impress others is through bragging, or boasting loudly of how different and blessed they are as compared to others. The subjects about which young people may brag are often varied. Some boast of the wide selection of clothes they may have, or about their house, or parents' achievements in life. It may be rather an unbecoming method of showing off, but when the audience is immature, it often works. The effect may not be lasting unless backed by truth. However, many young people are easily 'taken in' by such bragging.

Formation of Groups

Human nature is such that people who have similar thoughts and values are attracted to each other. This is exactly what happens when young people make friends in schools and colleges. They are naturally drawn into groups. Once this happens, besides the efforts to gain popularity, one begins to work within the group. One group may try to be better than another. The groups consist of boys, or girls, or may be mixed. It may be of young people living on the same street, or area, or studying in the same class. Groups may also be formed of young people coming from families with similar values and financial position. Members of such groups are usually of the same age.

Group loyalties are often very strong. The leadership is respected. Sometimes a person also goes against personal values just to be one of the group. Members of such groups cherish similar ideas about the type of clothes to wear, recreation, studies, and life in general. This gives them a sense of belonging outside the immediate family circle. It gives them status. Sometimes group loyalties become so strong that even parental wishes may be set aside in favour of group loyalties. However, this is only a transitory phase of growing up. Family ties are often stronger. Such groups can also lead one to baser forms of winning popularity as through brute physical strength, or experimentation with tobacco, alcohol, drugs and sex.

The Role of Money

With young people gaining greater awareness of the role of money and material possessions in life, many consider it an easy way to win immediate attention and even recognition. One would be wise to understand that the influence money or material possessions can exert on others to win popularity is extremely limited. It should not be given undue importance.

This can adversely affect money values in adult life.

Popularity Through One's Work

Intelligent young people know the true worth of working efficiently. Work has rightly been compared to worship. It immediately reflects one's ability to shoulder responsibilities, and one's devotion to duty. A work well done also reflects one's personal integrity, and honesty of purpose. These qualities are always appreciated and recognised. They have rightly motivated many young people to excel in their school and college work, at games and other activities. The process of gaining popularity this way is certainly slow, but once it is gained, it becomes a part of the person for a lifetime. The appreciation one gains this way is very satisfying. The only limitation is that the popularity one gains is limited to that sphere of activity in which one excels. This can well be overcome through balanced individual development.

Personal Attractiveness

Most young people believe that if nature has endowed them with an attractive face and body, or if they can make it so with modern make-up techniques and dress, they have little else to worry about to draw immediate attention. While it is true that personal attractiveness is a great blessing, by itself it can achieve nothing more than perhaps a second glance. To be truly attractive, one needs to cultivate personal charm, which does not come only from personal grooming, but from the many hidden qualities buried deep within each one of us. When developed, these qualities add on to an individual the vitality to hold attention, and be accepted as an attractive person.

Friendliness

The most prized quality to win popularity amongst people is friendliness. To develop this quality, one needs to be sincere, polite and gentle in one's dealings with others. One should be thoughtful of others' feelings, and should readily be willing to do favours, rather than ask for them. Such qualities cannot be developed overnight. They are the result of continued effort over several years. People who have won true popularity understand the need for a smiling face, personal charm, and etiquette and good manners in interpersonal relationships. The friendly person does not tell others why they should like him. Instead, he tells them why he likes them. He is honest, good-natured, and radiates optimism. He does not live for himself alone. He shares his life with others. Such are the qualities that help one win immediate attention, recognition and popularity.

Points to ponder...

- ❑ It is natural to desire appreciation.
- ❑ Some adults often serve as role models.
- ❑ Try to assess and understand human strengths and weaknesses.
- ❑ Adopt the positive. Avoid the negative.
- ❑ Be a friend.
- ❑ Do not chase popularity. It should come to you.

Books on Personality Development

Etiquette and good manners distinguish every gentleman and woman. Courtesies are an indispensable part of a civilised society at home, workplace or society and help ensure cordial relations amongst people.

Etiquette and manners are not instinctive, however, and need to be learnt. While many parents, elders and teachers make the effort to inculcate the basic courtesies in youngsters, it is humanly impossible to cover all aspects and situations of etiquette. This is a void that **The Book of Etiquette and Manners** fills in perfectly which is what makes this book indispensable reading for parents, elders, teachers and youngsters.

Topics include:

❖ Social etiquette ❖ Office etiquette ❖ Business etiquette ❖ Job-hunting etiquette ❖ Hospital etiquette ❖ Etiquette at Weddings ❖ Etiquette in Places of Worship ❖ E-mail etiquette ...And lots more.

A book for the young men and women, specially students, with Indian precepts and culture

This book seeks to motivate young men and women, particularly students, to make conscious and continuous effort to build character and develop personality. With deep insight, the author has provided valuable guidelines and practical steps on matters of special interest to students. Further, he has given them the benefit of experience, his own as well as those of eminent persons.

Considering the significant role of teachers and parents and their responsibility in moulding young minds, it is hoped that this book will be welcomed by them too.
